I0016928

Object-Oriented Programming Exercises with C#

ISBN: 9798395554772

Copyright © 2023 by Haris Tsetsekas

Table of Contents

1. Movies

Let's create a program that handles movies and their ratings. We need to record the following information on movies:

- Title
- Director
- Duration (in minutes)
- Year of release

The Movie class should have a method that returns the movie's age, based on the current year and the release year.

For each Movie, we should also keep a number of Ratings, ranging from 0 to 5. Moreover, a Movie of type Movie should be able to calculate the average of the ratings.

In the main method, we should create a number of Movies, along with some ratings. Then, we should print the details of each movie, as well as the ratings average.

Proposed Solution

We begin with creating the Movie class:

```
namespace Movies
{
  public class Movie
  {
    private int _year;
    private int _duration;

    public string Name { get; set; }
    public int Year
    {
      get => _year;
      set {
        if (value > 1900)
          _year = value;
        else
          Console.WriteLine("invalid year value");
      }
    }
    public int Duration
    {
      get => _duration;
      set {
        if (value >= 0)
          _duration = value;
```

```
        else
            Console.WriteLine("invalid duration value");
        }
    }
    public string Director { get; set; }
    public List<int> Reviews { get; set; }

...
    }
}
```

Listing 1-1: Movie.cs

The Movie class contains four properties; two of them are backed by two private variables (_year and _duration) so that we can define setter methods that check for correct values. For the other three properties we use the short-hand notation.

Then, we add three constructors, the default, the full and the copy constructor:

```
public Movie()
{
    Name = "N/A";
    Year = DateTime.Now.Year;
    Duration = 0;
    Director = "N/A";
    Reviews = new List<int>();
}

public Movie(string name, int year, int duration, String director)
{
    Name = name;
    Year = year;
    Duration = duration;
    Director = director;
    Reviews = new List<int>();
}

public Movie(Movie movie)
{
    Name = movie.Name;
    Year = movie.Year;
    Duration = movie.Duration;
    Director = movie.Director;
    Reviews = new List<int>(movie.Reviews);
}
```

Listing 1-2: Movie.cs

Note that the copy constructor is not provided by default in C#; we will have to introduce it ourselves. Moreover, in the copy constructor, we instantiate the Reviews list by using the List<> copy constructor.

With regard to the `Reviews` list, we add two methods; one to insert a review in the list and another one to calculate the average score:

```
public void AddReview(int score)
{
  if (score >= 0 && score <= 5)
    Reviews.Add(score);
  else
    Console.WriteLine("invalid review score");
}

public decimal GetReviewAverage()
{
  decimal sum = 0.0M;
  for (int i = 0; i < Reviews.Count(); i++)
    sum += Reviews.ElementAt(i);

  if (Reviews.Count() > 0)
    return decimal.Round(sum / Reviews.Count(), 1);
  else
    return 0;
}
```

Listing 1-3: Movie.cs

Next, we add a method to calculate the movie's age:

```
public int GetAge()
{
  int current_year = DateTime.Now.Year;
  return current_year - Year;
}
```

Listing 1-4: Movie.cs

In order to get the current year from the system, we use the `DateTime.Now.Year` property.

Finally, we add a `ToString()` method that provides a string representation of the `Movie` object:

```
public override string ToString()
{
  string reviews = "";
  foreach (var r in Reviews)
    reviews = reviews + r.ToString() + ",";

  if (reviews.Length > 0)
    reviews = reviews.Substring(0, reviews.Length - 1);

  return "Movie{" +
      "name='" + Name + '\'' +
      ", year=" + Year +
      ", duration=" + Duration +
      ", director='" + Director + '\'' +
```

```
        ", reviews=" + reviews +
        ", reviews average=" + GetReviewAverage() +
        '}';
    }
```

Listing 1-5: Movie.cs

In the `Main` method, we create some `Movie` objects and we test their functionality:

```
namespace Movies
{
    public class Program
    {
        public static void Main(string[] args)
        {
            Movie m1 = new Movie();
            Movie m2 = new Movie("Hunger Games", 2012, 142, "Gary Ross");
            m2.AddReview(5);
            m2.AddReview(4);
            m2.AddReview(6);

            Movie m3 = new Movie(m2);
            m3.AddReview(2);
            Console.WriteLine(m1);
            Console.WriteLine(m2);
            Console.WriteLine(m3);
        }
    }
}
```

Listing 1-6: Movie.cs

You can find this project in GitHub:

https://github.com/htset/csharp_oop_exercises/tree/master/Movies

2. Hospital

In this project, we will create a console application that will manage patients in a hospital.

The hospital consists of clinics (e.g. surgery). We should keep track of the clinic's name and its director's name.

For each patient, we will maintain the following information:

- Patient name and surname
- Year of birth
- The clinic in which the patient has been admitted to
- Room number
- A list of measurements (temperature and measurement date/time)

The patient class should be able to return the maximum temperature recorded for a patient. It should also display the full information on a patient (and the respective clinic).

In the main method, we should create a number of clinics and patients, as well as add some measurements to each patient. Next, we should be able to change the name of the director of a clinic, as well as move a patient to a new clinic.

Proposed Solution

We begin with the definition of the `Clinic` class:

```
namespace Hospital
{
  public class Clinic
  {
    public string Name { get; set; }
    public string Director { get; set; }

    public Clinic(string name, string director)
    {
      Name = name;
      Director = director;
    }

    public Clinic()
    {
      Name = "N/A";
      Director = "N/A";
    }
    public override string ToString()
    {
      return "Clinic{" +
          "name='" + Name + '\'' +
          ", director='" + Director + '\'' +
```

```
            '}';
        }
    }
}
```

Listing 2-1: Clinic.cs

We proceed with the definition of the Patient class:

```
namespace Hospital
{
  public class Patient
  {
    public string Name { get; set; }
    public string Surname { get; set; }
    public int YearOfBirth { get; set; }
    public Clinic? Clinic { get; set; }
    public string Room { get; set; }
    public List<Measurement> Measurements { get; set; }
    ...
  }
}
```

Listing 2-2: Patient.cs

There are two things worth mentioning here: First of all, the Patient object keeps a reference to a Clinic object. The Clinic object exists independently of the Patient object, as there are many patients that may belong to the same clinic. This is an example of *Aggregation*: we keep references to external objects that are related to the object in question.

The opposite of *Aggregation* is *Composition*: it's when an object contains other objects inside it. This is the case of the Measurement list. The temperature taken for a patient is strongly connected to the patient and does not make any sense without one. If the patient object is deleted, it is OK to delete also the temperature information.

Let's get the definition of the simple Measurement class out of the way:

```
namespace Hospital
{
  public class Measurement
  {
    public double Temp { get; set; }
    public DateTime Date { get; set; }

    public Measurement(double temp, DateTime date)
    {
      Temp = temp;
      Date = date;
    }

    public Measurement()
    {
```

```
        Temp = 0;
        Date = DateTime.Now;
    }

    public override string ToString()
    {
        return "Measurement{" +
            "temp=" + Temp +
            ", date=" + Date +
            '}';
    }
}
}
```

Listing 2-3: Measurement.cs

Now, for the implementation of the Patient class, first we add the constructors:

```
public Patient(string name, string surname, int yearOfBirth, Clinic clinic, string
room)
{
    Name = name;
    Surname = surname;
    YearOfBirth = yearOfBirth;
    Clinic = clinic;
    Room = room;
    Measurements = new List<Measurement>();
}

public Patient()
{
    Name = "N/A";
    Surname = "N/A";
    YearOfBirth = 0;
    Clinic = null;
    Room = "N/A";
    Measurements = new List<Measurement>();
}
```

Listing 2-4: Patient.cs

Then, we have the two methods for Measurement insertion:

```
public void insertMeasurement(Measurement m)
{
    Measurements.Add(m);
}

public void insertMeasurement(double temp, DateTime date)
{
    var m = new Measurement(temp, date);
    Measurements.Add(m);
}
```

Listing 2-5: Patient.cs

Next, we implement a `ToString()` method, as well as the methods to get the maximum recorded temperature and the age of the patient:

```csharp
public double maxTemp()
{
  double maxtemp = 0.0;
  foreach (var m in Measurements)
  {
    if (m.Temp > maxtemp)
      maxtemp = m.Temp;
  }
  return maxtemp;
}

public override string ToString()
{
  var measurements = "";
  foreach (var m in Measurements)
    measurements = measurements + m.ToString() + ",";

  if (measurements.Length > 0)
    measurements = measurements.Substring(0, measurements.Length - 1);

  return "Patient{" +
      "name='" + Name + '\'' +
      ", surname='" + Surname + '\'' +
      ", yearOfBirth=" + YearOfBirth +
      ", clinic=" + Clinic +
      ", room='" + Room + '\'' +
      ", pm=[" + measurements +
      "]}";
}

public int GetAge()
{
  return DateTime.Now.Year - YearOfBirth;
}
```

Listing 2-6: Patient.cs

Finally, in the `Main()` method, we define a number of clinics, patients and measurements. Note how we change the name of the surgery clinic director in one place. Moreover, we can move a patient to another clinic simply by assigning the reference of a different `Clinic` object:

```csharp
namespace Hospital
{
  public class Program
  {
    static void Main(string[] args)
    {
      Clinic c1 = new Clinic("Surgery", "A. Dobbs");
      Clinic c2 = new Clinic("Cardiology", "B. Smith");
```

```csharp
    Clinic c3 = new Clinic("Orthopedics", "C. Stubbs");

    Patient p1 = new Patient("John", "Doe", 1970, c1, "303");
    Patient p2 = new Patient("Jane", "Doe", 1985, c2, "306");
    Patient p3 = new Patient("Jimmy", "Doe", 1956, c2, "306");

    p1.insertMeasurement(new Measurement(37.5,
        new DateTime(2023, 1, 1, 0, 0, 0)));
    p1.insertMeasurement(new Measurement(38.1,
        new DateTime(2023, 1, 1, 6, 0, 0)));
    p1.insertMeasurement(new Measurement(37.9,
        new DateTime(2023, 1, 1, 9, 0, 0)));

    p2.insertMeasurement(new Measurement(36.5,
        new DateTime(2023, 1, 1, 0, 0, 0)));
    p2.insertMeasurement(new Measurement(38.0,
        new DateTime(2023, 1, 1, 6, 0, 0)));

    p3.insertMeasurement(new Measurement(39.5,
        new DateTime(2023, 1, 1, 0, 0, 0)));
    p3.insertMeasurement(new Measurement(39.1,
        new DateTime(2023, 1, 1, 6, 0, 0)));

    p3.Clinic = c3;
    c1.Director = "D. Jones";

    Console.WriteLine(p1);
    Console.WriteLine(p2);
    Console.WriteLine(p3);
    }
  }
}
```

Listing 2-7: Hospital.cs

You can find this project in GitHub:

https://github.com/htset/csharp_oop_exercises/tree/master/Hospital

3. Package Shipping

Let's create a class hierarchy that models the different type of packages provided by a shipping company. There are three package types, with different costs and delivery times:

- Base package: Costs €5 per kilo and is delivered in 5 days. If the package weight is more than 10 kilos, then one more day is required
- Advanced package: Costs €6 per kilo with an additional €2 fee. The package is delivered after 2 days.
- Overnight package: Delivered the next day and costs €10 per kilo

In the main method, we should be able insert packages of all kinds in the same array. At the end, we should print all packages in a loop.

Proposed Solution

First, we create an *abstract base class* as the root of the package hierarchy:

```
namespace PackageShipping
{
  public abstract class Package
  {
    private double _weight;
    public string Recipient { get; set; }
    public string Address { get; set; }
    public double Weight
    {
      get => _weight;
      set
      {
        if (value < 0)
          throw new Exception("Weight should be >= 0");
        else
          _weight = value;
      }
    }
    public DateTime ShipmentDate { get; set; }

    public Package(string recipient, string address, double weight,
                DateTime shipmentDate)
    {
      Recipient = recipient;
      Address = address;
      Weight = weight;
      ShipmentDate = shipmentDate;
    }

    public Package()
    {
      Recipient = "";
```

```
        Address = "";
        Weight = 0;
        ShipmentDate = DateTime.Now;
    }

    public abstract double CalculateCost();

    public abstract DateTime CalculateDeliveryDate();
  }
}
```

Listing 3-1: Package.cs

Class `Package` defines two *abstract methods* that should be implemented by derived classes:

- CalculateCost()
- CalculateDeliveryDate()

The `BasePackage` class implements the simple version of package shipping:

```
namespace PackageShipping
{
  public class BasePackage : Package
  {
    public BasePackage(string recipient, string address, double weight,
      DateTime shipmentDate) : base(recipient, address, weight, shipmentDate)
    { }

    public BasePackage() : base()
    { }

    public override double CalculateCost()
    {
      return Constants.BASE_PACKAGE_COST_FACTOR * Weight;
    }

    public override DateTime CalculateDeliveryDate()
    {
      if (Weight <= Constants.BASE_PACKAGE_MAX_WEIGHT)
        return ShipmentDate.AddDays(Constants.BASE_PACKAGE_DAYS);
      else
        return ShipmentDate.AddDays(Constants.BASE_PACKAGE_DAYS + 1);
    }
  }
}
```

Listing 3-2: BasePackage.cs

The constants are contained inside a special class called `Constants`:

```
namespace PackageShipping
{
  public class Constants
  {
```

```
    public const int BASE_PACKAGE_COST_FACTOR = 5;
    public const int BASE_PACKAGE_DAYS = 5;
    public const int BASE_PACKAGE_MAX_WEIGHT = 10;
    public const int ADVANCED_PACKAGE_COST_FACTOR = 5;
    public const int ADVANCED_PACKAGE_COST_SUPPL = 2;
    public const int ADVANCED_PACKAGE_DAYS = 2;
    public const int OVERNIGHT_PACKAGE_COST_FACTOR = 10;
    public const int OVERNIGHT_PACKAGE_DAYS = 1;
  }
}
```

Listing 3-3: Constants.cs

AdvancedPackage class is a bit different, with regard to the implementation of the two abstract methods:

```
namespace PackageShipping
{
  public class AdvancedPackage : Package
  {
    public AdvancedPackage(String recipient, string address, double weight,
      DateTime shipmentDate) : base(recipient, address, weight, shipmentDate)
    { }

    public AdvancedPackage() : base()
    { }

    public override double CalculateCost()
    {
      return Constants.ADVANCED_PACKAGE_COST_FACTOR * Weight
          + Constants.ADVANCED_PACKAGE_COST_SUPPL;
    }

    public override DateTime CalculateDeliveryDate()
    {
      return ShipmentDate.AddDays(Constants.ADVANCED_PACKAGE_DAYS);
    }
  }
}
```

Listing 3-4: AdvancedPackage.cs

Also, we implement the OvernightPackage class:

```
namespace PackageShipping
{
  public class OvernightPackage : Package
  {
    public OvernightPackage(String recipient, string address, double weight,
      DateTime shipmentDate) : base(recipient, address, weight, shipmentDate)
    { }

    public OvernightPackage() : base()
    { }
```

```csharp
    public override double CalculateCost()
    {
      return Constants.OVERNIGHT_PACKAGE_COST_FACTOR * Weight;
    }

    public override DateTime CalculateDeliveryDate()
    {
      return ShipmentDate.AddDays(Constants.OVERNIGHT_PACKAGE_DAYS);
    }
  }
}
```

Listing 3-5: OvernightPackage.cs

The importance of polymorphism can be realized in the `Main()` method:

```csharp
namespace PackageShipping
{
  public class Program
  {
    public static void Main(string[] args)
    {
      var packages = new Package[4];

      packages[0] = new BasePackage("John Doe", "12 Main str.", 15,
          new DateTime(2023, 1, 12));
      packages[1] = new BasePackage("Jane Doe", "1 High str.", 9.5,
          new DateTime(2022, 12, 30));
      packages[2] = new AdvancedPackage("Janet Doe", "3 Square dr.", 15,
          new DateTime(2023, 1, 12));
      packages[3] = new OvernightPackage("James Doe", "12 Infinite loop", 1,
          new DateTime(2023, 1, 20));

      int i = 1;
      foreach (var p in packages)
      {
        Console.WriteLine("Package no." + i++);
        Console.WriteLine("Type: " + p.GetType());
        Console.WriteLine("Delivery date: " + p.CalculateDeliveryDate());
        Console.WriteLine("Cost: " + p.CalculateCost() + "\n");
      }
    }
  }
}
```

Listing 3-6: Program.cs

Here, we define an array (could also be a `List`) that contains references to `Package` objects. This means that we can also use this array to contain references to objects that *derive* from `Package`, such as `BasePackage`. In this way, we are able to store objects of different types (but with a common ancestor) into the same array, and treat them uniformly.

Also note how we can find out the type of the object that is pointed to:

```
p.getType()
```

When p references a `BasePackage` object then the result will be `PackageShipping.BasePackage` (the namespace is also included).

You can find this project in GitHub:

https://github.com/htset/csharp_oop_exercises/tree/master/PackageShipping

4. Package Shipping with Persistence

We will continue with the package shipping project with the following improvements:

- User interaction: Users should be able to add and delete packages, search for packages (based on the name of the recipient) and list all available packages.
- File persistence: Packages should be saved into a single file. Also, when the application starts, the packages should be loaded from the file.

Proposed Solution

First of all, let's see how the `Main()` method will now appear:

```
namespace PackageShipping
{
  public class Program
  {
    public static void Main(string[] args)
    {
      try
      {
        var list = new List<Package>();
        var ui = new UIService(list);
        ui.LoadFromFile();
        ui.Menu();
      }
      catch (IOException ioe)
      {
        Console.WriteLine("IO Exception!");
        Console.WriteLine(ioe.StackTrace);
        System.Environment.Exit(1);
      }
    }
  }
}
```

Listing 4-1: Program.cs

Here, we define a `List` that will contain references to `Package` objects (and its derived classes). We also define a new class called `UIService` that will handle the interaction with the user. We pass the `List` to the constructor of the `UIService` class and we proceed with loading the packages from the text file. Then, the `Menu()` method handles all the interaction with the user.

The `UIService` class is (partially) defined here:

```
namespace PackageShipping
{
  public class UIService
  {
```

```
    private List<Package> Packages;

    public UIService(List<Package> packages)
    {
      Packages = packages;
    }
  ...
  }
}
```

Listing 4-2: UIService.cs

In the constructor of the class, we store the reference to the Package list; we will use it in the following methods.

The Menu() method maintains a loop and provides the options to the user:

```
public void Menu()
{
  int option;
  do
  {
    Console.WriteLine("Options: ");
    Console.WriteLine("1) Add package ");
    Console.WriteLine("2) Search package ");
    Console.WriteLine("3) Delete package ");
    Console.WriteLine("4) View all packages ");
    Console.WriteLine("0) Exit ");

    int.TryParse(Console.ReadLine(), out option);

    switch (option)
    {
      case 1:
        AddPackage();
        break;
      case 2:
        SearchPackage();
        break;
      case 3:
        DeletePackage();
        break;
      case 4:
        ListPackages();
        break;
      case 0:
        break;
      default:
        Console.WriteLine("Please type again:");
        break;
    }
  } while (option != 0);
}
```

Listing 4-3: UIService.cs

For simplicity and to make the core concepts of the exercise more visible, we refrain from making extensive checks on the user input. Here, we just use TryParse to convert the string input to an integer. If the user types a character then TryParse returns 0, so the program ends. In the following snippets, we just use Convert.ToInt32() for parsing, without any exception checking.

Next, the AddPackage() method gets the package information from the user, creates the selected type of Package and inserts it into the list:

```csharp
private void AddPackage()
{
    int option;
    string? recipient_name, recipient_address;
    double weight;

    Console.WriteLine("Type of package (1-Basic, 2-Advanced, 3-Overnight)");
    option = Convert.ToInt32(Console.ReadLine());
    Console.WriteLine("Recipient name: ");
    recipient_name = Console.ReadLine() ?? "";
    Console.WriteLine("Recipient address: ");
    recipient_address = Console.ReadLine() ?? "";
    Console.WriteLine("Weight (kilos):");
    weight = Convert.ToDouble(Console.ReadLine());
    switch (option)
    {
        case 1:
            Packages.Add(new BasePackage(recipient_name, recipient_address,
                weight, DateTime.Now));
            SaveToFile();
            break;
        case 2:
            Packages.Add(new AdvancedPackage(recipient_name, recipient_address,
                weight, DateTime.Now));
            SaveToFile();
            break;
        case 3:
            Packages.Add(new OvernightPackage(recipient_name, recipient_address,
                weight, DateTime.Now));
            SaveToFile();
            break;
        default:
            break;
    }
}
```

Listing 4-4: UIService.cs

Note how we create new packages on the fly and how we pass their references to the list.

We can search for a package (or packages) based on the recipient's name and print all the details:

```csharp
private void SearchPackage()
{
  string? recipient_name;
  Console.WriteLine("Enter recipient name (also partial): ");
  recipient_name = Console.ReadLine() ?? "";

  foreach (var p in Packages)
  {
    if (p.Recipient.IndexOf(recipient_name) >= 0)
    {
      Console.WriteLine(p);
    }
  }
}
```

Listing 4-5: UIService.cs

In order to delete a package, we first search for it, based on the recipient's name. We then ask the user to select from a list the package to be deleted:

```csharp
private void DeletePackage()
{
  string recipient_name;
  Console.Write("Enter recipient name (also partial): ");
  recipient_name = Console.ReadLine()?? "";

  int i = 0;
  Console.WriteLine("The following packages were found:");
  foreach (var p in Packages)
  {
    if (p.Recipient.IndexOf(recipient_name) >= 0)
    {
      Console.WriteLine("Package no. " + (i + 1) + ":");
      Console.WriteLine(p);
    }
    i++;
  }

  int option;
  Console.WriteLine("Please enter the no. of package to delete (0 to cancel): ");
  option = Convert.ToInt32(Console.ReadLine());

  if (option > 0)
  {
    Packages.RemoveAt(option - 1);
    Console.WriteLine("package deleted");
    SaveToFile();
  }
}
```

Listing 4-6: UIService.cs

The ListPackages() method simply prints all the packages in the list:

```
private void ListPackages()
{
  foreach (var p in Packages)
  {
    Console.WriteLine(p);
  }
}
```

Listing 4-7: UIService.cs

Now, it's time to see the file handling methods. When a new package is inserted (or deleted), we update the text file that we use to store the packages. File handling in C# is not easy; there is no straightforward way to insert some text in the middle of a file, in a way that the remaining text is pushed to the end to make space of the new text.

What we choose to do here, is to clear the file and re-write it when a package is added or removed. This is what SaveToFile() does:

```
private void SaveToFile()
{
  using (var writer = new StreamWriter("packages.txt"))
  {
    foreach (var p in Packages)
    {
      writer.WriteLine(p.Serialize());
    }
  }
}
```

Listing 4-8: UIService.cs

On startup, we load the package information stored in the file, we create the packages one by one and store them in the list:

```
public void LoadFromFile()
{
  Packages.Clear();

  if (!File.Exists("packages.txt"))
  {
    var newFile = File.Create("packages.txt");
    newFile.Close();
  }

  using (var reader = new StreamReader("packages.txt"))
  {
    string line;
    string? package_str = "";
    while ((line = reader.ReadLine()) != null)
    {
      if (line.IndexOf("--") == 0)
      {
        Package p;
```

```
            if (package_str.IndexOf("Base Package") == 0)
            {
              p = new BasePackage();
              p.Deserialize(package_str);
              Packages.Add(p);
            }
            else if (package_str.IndexOf("Advanced Package") == 0)
            {
              p = new AdvancedPackage();
              p.Deserialize(package_str);
              Packages.Add(p);
            }
            else if (package_str.IndexOf("Overnight Package") == 0)
            {
              p = new OvernightPackage();
              p.Deserialize(package_str);
              Packages.Add(p);
            }
            else
            {
              Console.WriteLine("error loading packages. Exiting..");
              System.Environment.Exit(1);
            }
            package_str = "";
          }
          else
          {
            package_str += line + "\n";
          }
        }
      }
    }
```

Listing 4-9: UIService.cs

The entry of each package has the following form (here for `AdvancedPackage`):

```
Advanced Package
John Doe
1 Main str. Boston
11.3
27/12/2022
--
```

Listing 4-10: text file

Note that the entries are separated by two dashes (--) and that on the first line of the entry we get the type of the package.

With that out of the way, we can proceed with the definition of the `Package` class:

```
namespace PackageShipping
{
  public abstract class Package
  {
```

```
    private double _weight;
    public string Recipient { get; set; }
    public string Address { get; set; }
    public double Weight
    {
      get => _weight;
      set
      {
        if (value < 0)
          throw new Exception("Weight should be >= 0");
        else
          _weight = value;
      }
    }
    public DateTime ShipmentDate { get; set; }


    public Package(string recipient, string address, double weight,
                DateTime shipmentDate)
    {
      Recipient = recipient;
      Address = address;
      Weight = weight;
      ShipmentDate = shipmentDate;
    }

    public Package()
    {
      Recipient = "";
      Address = "";
      Weight = 0;
      ShipmentDate = DateTime.Now;
    }

    public abstract double CalculateCost();
    public abstract DateTime CalculateDeliveryDate();
    public override abstract string ToString();
    public abstract string Serialize();
    public abstract void Deserialize(string s);
  }
}
```

Listing 4-11: Package.cs

In comparison to the previous project, we have added two new abstract methods,
Serialize() and Deserialize(), that handle writing and reading the package from the text
file. We have also added another method (ToString()) that returns a string representation
of a package object to be used for console output.

Now, let's see the BasePackage class definition:

```
using System.Text;
using System.Text.RegularExpressions;
```

```csharp
namespace PackageShipping
{
  public class BasePackage : Package
  {
    public BasePackage(string recipient, string address, double weight,
      DateTime shipmentDate) : base(recipient, address, weight, shipmentDate)
    { }

    public BasePackage() : base()
    { }

    public override double CalculateCost()
    {
      return Constants.BASE_PACKAGE_COST_FACTOR * Weight;
    }

    public override DateTime CalculateDeliveryDate()
    {
      if (Weight <= Constants.BASE_PACKAGE_MAX_WEIGHT)
        return ShipmentDate.AddDays(Constants.BASE_PACKAGE_DAYS);
      else
        return ShipmentDate.AddDays(Constants.BASE_PACKAGE_DAYS + 1);
    }

    public override string ToString()
    {
      var str = new StringBuilder();
      str.Append("\n--Base Package--");
      str.Append("\nRecipient: " + Recipient);
      str.Append("\nAddress: " + Address);
      str.Append("\nWeight: " + Weight);
      str.Append("\nShipment date:" + ShipmentDate);
      str.Append("\nExpected delivery date:" + CalculateDeliveryDate());
      str.Append("\nCost:" + CalculateCost());
      str.Append("\n--------------------");
      return str.ToString();
    }

    public override string Serialize()
    {
      var str = new StringBuilder();
      str.Append("Base Package\n");
      str.Append(Recipient + "\n");
      str.Append(Address + "\n");
      str.Append(Weight + "\n");
      str.Append(ShipmentDate + "\n");
      str.Append("--");
      return str.ToString();
    }

    public override void Deserialize(string s)
    {
      var regex = new Regex("\n");
      var lines = regex.Split(s);
```

```
      Recipient = lines[1];
      Address = lines[2];
      Weight = Double.Parse(lines[3]);
      ShipmentDate = DateTime.Parse(lines[4]);
    }
  }
}
```

Listing 4-12: BasePackage.cs

In first two of the added methods, we use the StringBuilder class that provides us with a buffer in order to build a string in successive calls. In the third method, we use Regular Expressions to split the string based on newline characters, so that each line will be inserted into a different position in the string array.

The implementation of the AdvancedPackage and OvernightPackage classes are similar to the BasePackage one. We provide them here for completeness.

```
using System.Text;
using System.Text.RegularExpressions;

namespace PackageShipping
{
  public class AdvancedPackage : Package
  {
    public AdvancedPackage(string recipient, string address, double weight,
      DateTime shipmentDate) : base(recipient, address, weight, shipmentDate)
    { }

    public AdvancedPackage() : base()
    { }

    public override double CalculateCost()
    {
      return Constants.ADVANCED_PACKAGE_COST_FACTOR * Weight
          + Constants.ADVANCED_PACKAGE_COST_SUPPL;
    }

    public override DateTime CalculateDeliveryDate()
    {
      return ShipmentDate.AddDays(Constants.ADVANCED_PACKAGE_DAYS);
    }

    public override string ToString()
    {
      var str = new StringBuilder();
      str.Append("\n--Advanced Package--");
      str.Append("\nRecipient: " + Recipient);
      str.Append("\nAddress: " + Address);
      str.Append("\nWeight: " + Weight);
      str.Append("\nShipment date:" + ShipmentDate);
      str.Append("\nExpected delivery date:" + CalculateDeliveryDate());
```

```csharp
      str.Append("\nCost:" + CalculateCost());
      str.Append("\n--------------------");
      return str.ToString();
    }

    public override string Serialize()
    {
      var str = new StringBuilder();
      str.Append("Advanced Package\n");
      str.Append(Recipient + "\n");
      str.Append(Address + "\n");
      str.Append(Weight + "\n");
      str.Append(ShipmentDate + "\n");
      str.Append("--");
      return str.ToString();
    }

    public override void Deserialize(string s)
    {
      var regex = new Regex("\n");
      var lines = regex.Split(s);

      Recipient = lines[1];
      Address = lines[2];
      Weight = Double.Parse(lines[3]);
      ShipmentDate = DateTime.Parse(lines[4]);
    }
  }
}
```

Listing 4-13: AdvancedPackage.cs

```csharp
using System.Text;
using System.Text.RegularExpressions;

namespace PackageShipping
{
  public class OvernightPackage : Package
  {
    public OvernightPackage(string recipient, string address, double weight,
      DateTime shipmentDate) : base(recipient, address, weight, shipmentDate)
    { }

    public OvernightPackage() : base()
    { }

    public override double CalculateCost()
    {
      return Constants.OVERNIGHT_PACKAGE_COST_FACTOR * Weight;
    }

    public override DateTime CalculateDeliveryDate()
    {
```

```csharp
            return ShipmentDate.AddDays(Constants.OVERNIGHT_PACKAGE_DAYS);
        }

        public override string ToString()
        {
            var str = new StringBuilder();
            str.Append("\n--Overnight Package--");
            str.Append("\nRecipient: " + Recipient);
            str.Append("\nAddress: " + Address);
            str.Append("\nWeight: " + Weight);
            str.Append("\nShipment date:" + ShipmentDate);
            str.Append("\nExpected delivery date:" + CalculateDeliveryDate());
            str.Append("\nCost:" + CalculateCost());
            str.Append("\n--------------------");
            return str.ToString();
        }

        public override string Serialize()
        {
            var str = new StringBuilder();
            str.Append("Overnight Package\n");
            str.Append(Recipient + "\n");
            str.Append(Address + "\n");
            str.Append(Weight + "\n");
            str.Append(ShipmentDate + "\n");
            str.Append("--");
            return str.ToString();
        }

        public override void Deserialize(string s)
        {
            var regex = new Regex("\n");
            var lines = regex.Split(s);

            Recipient = lines[1];
            Address = lines[2];
            Weight = Double.Parse(lines[3]);
            ShipmentDate = DateTime.Parse(lines[4]);
        }
    }
}
```

Listing 4-14: OvernightPackage.cs

You can find this project in GitHub:

https://github.com/htset/csharp_oop_exercises/tree/master/PackageShippingFiles

5. Package Shipping with GUI

Here we will continue the previous exercise by creating a simple GUI using the Windows Presentation Framework (WPF). This GUI will do the following:

- Present a list of all created packages in the system
- Provide the option to insert a new package

Proposed Solution

In the previous version of the Package Shipping exercise, the console-based UI class handled both the interaction with the user and the data storage in the text file. Here, we will separate the file handling functionality in a new class, named `PersistenceService`:

```csharp
using System;
using System.Collections.Generic;
using System.IO;

namespace PackageShippingGUI
{
  public class PersistenceService
  {
    private List<Package> Packages;

    public PersistenceService(List<Package> packages)
    {
      Packages = packages;
    }

    public void SaveToFile()
    {
      using (var writer = new StreamWriter("packages.txt"))
      {
        foreach (var p in Packages)
        {
          writer.WriteLine(p.Serialize());
        }
      }
    }

    public void LoadFromFile()
    {
      Packages.Clear();

      if (!File.Exists("packages.txt"))
      {
        var newFile = File.Create("packages.txt");
        newFile.Close();
      }

      using (var reader = new StreamReader("packages.txt"))
```

```csharp
    {
      string line;
      string? package_str = "";
      while ((line = reader.ReadLine()) != null)
      {
        if (line.IndexOf("--") == 0)
        {
          Package p;
          if (package_str.IndexOf("Base Package") == 0)
          {
            p = new BasePackage();
            p.Deserialize(package_str);
            Packages.Add(p);
          }
          else if (package_str.IndexOf("Advanced Package") == 0)
          {
            p = new AdvancedPackage();
            p.Deserialize(package_str);
            Packages.Add(p);
          }
          else if (package_str.IndexOf("Overnight Package") == 0)
          {
            p = new OvernightPackage();
            p.Deserialize(package_str);
            Packages.Add(p);
          }
          else
          {
            Console.WriteLine("error loading packages. Exiting..");
            System.Environment.Exit(1);
          }
          package_str = "";
        }
        else
        {
          package_str += line + "\n";
        }
      }
    }
  }
}
```

Listing 5-1: PersistenceService.cs

The PersistenceService class receives a package list as input parameter and populates it in method LoadFromFile(). Conversely, it stores all its contents in the same file in method SaveToFile().

The package list is defined in the main class (MainWindow) and its reference is passed to the other classes:

```csharp
using System;
using System.Collections.Generic;
```

```csharp
using System.Linq;
using System.Windows;
using System.Windows.Controls;
using System.Windows.Data;

namespace PackageShippingGUI
{
  public partial class MainWindow : Window
  {
    private List<Package> Packages;
    private PersistenceService Ps;

    public MainWindow()
    {
      InitializeComponent();

      var c1 = new DataGridTextColumn();
      c1.Header = "Package Type";
      c1.Binding = new Binding("PackageType");
      c1.Width = 110;
      packageGrid.Columns.Add(c1);
      var c2 = new DataGridTextColumn();
      c2.Header = "Recipient";
      c2.Width = 110;
      c2.Binding = new Binding("Recipient");
      packageGrid.Columns.Add(c2);
      var c3 = new DataGridTextColumn();
      c3.Header = "Address";
      c3.Width = 110;
      c3.Binding = new Binding("Address");
      packageGrid.Columns.Add(c3);
      var c4 = new DataGridTextColumn();
      c4.Header = "Weight";
      c4.Width = 110;
      c4.Binding = new Binding("Weight");
      packageGrid.Columns.Add(c4);
      var c5 = new DataGridTextColumn();
      c5.Header = "Shipment Date";
      c5.Width = 110;
      c5.Binding = new Binding("ShipmentDate");
      packageGrid.Columns.Add(c5);
      var c6 = new DataGridTextColumn();
      c6.Header = "Cost";
      c6.Width = 110;
      c6.Binding = new Binding("Cost");
      packageGrid.Columns.Add(c6);
      var c7 = new DataGridTextColumn();
      c7.Header = "Delivery Date";
      c7.Width = 110;
      c7.Binding = new Binding("DeliveryDate");
      packageGrid.Columns.Add(c7);

      Packages = new List<Package>();
      Ps = new PersistenceService(Packages);
```

```
        Ps.LoadFromFile();
        PopulateGrid();
    }

    private void PopulateGrid()
    {
      packageGrid.Items.Clear();

      foreach (var p in Packages)
      {
        packageGrid.Items.Add(
            new
            {
              PackageType = p.GetType().Name
                .Substring(0, p.GetType().Name.IndexOf("Package")),
              Recipient = p.Recipient,
              Address = p.Address,
              Weight = p.Weight,
              ShipmentDate = p.ShipmentDate.ToShortDateString(),
              Cost = p.CalculateCost(),
              DeliveryDate = p.CalculateDeliveryDate().ToShortDateString()
            }
        );
      }
    }

    private void AddPackage_Click(object sender, RoutedEventArgs e)
    {
      var form = new PackageForm();
      form.ShowDialog();
      if (form.package != null)
      {
        Packages.Add(form.package);
        Ps.SaveToFile();
        PopulateGrid();
      }
    }
  }
}
```

Listing 5-2: MainWindow.cs

The MainWindow class presents users with a grid containing all the existing package
shipments so far. Here is the XAML code for the main window:

```
<Window x:Name="___No_Name_" x:Class="PackageShippingGUI.MainWindow"
        xmlns="http://schemas.microsoft.com/winfx/2006/xaml/presentation"
        xmlns:x="http://schemas.microsoft.com/winfx/2006/xaml"
        xmlns:d="http://schemas.microsoft.com/expression/blend/2008"
        xmlns:mc="http://schemas.openxmlformats.org/markup-compatibility/2006"
        xmlns:local="clr-namespace:PackageShippingGUI"
        mc:Ignorable="d"
        Title="Package Shipping GUI" Height="450" Width="800">
    <Grid>
        <Grid.ColumnDefinitions>
```

```
            <ColumnDefinition/>
        </Grid.ColumnDefinitions>
        <DataGrid x:Name="packageGrid" d:ItemsSource="{d:SampleData ItemCount=5}"
            Margin="0,48,0,0" IsReadOnly="True"/>
        <Button x:Name="AddPackage" Content="Add New Package"
            HorizontalAlignment="Left" Height="23" Margin="28,10,0,0"
            VerticalAlignment="Top" Width="106" Click="AddPackage_Click"/>
    </Grid>
</Window>
```

Listing 5-3: MainWindow.xaml

When the *Add new Package* button is pressed, a *modal* form is displayed for the user to fill in the details of the new package. Here is the XAML code of the PackageForm class:

```
<Window x:Class="PackageShippingGUI.PackageForm"
        xmlns="http://schemas.microsoft.com/winfx/2006/xaml/presentation"
        xmlns:x="http://schemas.microsoft.com/winfx/2006/xaml"
        xmlns:d="http://schemas.microsoft.com/expression/blend/2008"
        xmlns:mc="http://schemas.openxmlformats.org/markup-compatibility/2006"
        xmlns:local="clr-namespace:PackageShippingGUI"
        mc:Ignorable="d"
        Title="Package Details" Height="292" Width="476">
    <Grid>
        <ComboBox x:Name="PackageType" HorizontalAlignment="Left" Margin="198,25,0,0"
            VerticalAlignment="Top" Width="183"/>
        <Label Content="Package Type" HorizontalAlignment="Left" Margin="33,25,0,0"
            VerticalAlignment="Top"/>
        <Label Content="Recipient Name" HorizontalAlignment="Left" Margin="33,59,0,0"
            VerticalAlignment="Top"/>
        <TextBox x:Name="Recipient" HorizontalAlignment="Left" Margin="198,63,0,0"
            TextWrapping="Wrap" VerticalAlignment="Top" Width="183"/>
        <TextBox x:Name="Address" HorizontalAlignment="Left" Margin="198,96,0,0"
            TextWrapping="Wrap" VerticalAlignment="Top" Width="183"/>
        <TextBox x:Name="Weight" HorizontalAlignment="Left" Margin="198,127,0,0"
            TextWrapping="Wrap" VerticalAlignment="Top" Width="183"/>
        <DatePicker x:Name="ShipmentDate" HorizontalAlignment="Left"
            Margin="198,160,0,0" VerticalAlignment="Top" Width="183"/>
        <Label Content="Recipient Address" HorizontalAlignment="Left"
            Margin="33,92,0,0" VerticalAlignment="Top"/>
        <Label Content="Weight" HorizontalAlignment="Left" Margin="33,123,0,0"
            VerticalAlignment="Top"/>
        <Label Content="Shipment Date" HorizontalAlignment="Left" Margin="33,158,0,0"
            VerticalAlignment="Top"/>
        <Button x:Name="SaveButton" Content="Save" HorizontalAlignment="Center"
            Height="26" Margin="0,221,0,0" VerticalAlignment="Top" Width="80"
            Click="SaveButton_Click" RenderTransformOrigin="0.619,3.268"/>
    </Grid>
</Window>
```

Listing 5-4: PackageForm.xaml

When the *Save* button is clicked the SaveButton_click() method reads the user input from the Text Boxes. It then uses the input to create a new Package object and add it in the package list. The type of package depends on the selection on the *package type* drop-down list.

Here is the corresponding C# code:

```csharp
using System;
using System.Windows;

namespace PackageShippingGUI
{
  public partial class PackageForm : Window
  {
    public Package? package { get; set; }

    public PackageForm()
    {
      InitializeComponent();

      PackageType.Items.Clear();
      PackageType.Items.Add("Base");
      PackageType.Items.Add("Advanced");
      PackageType.Items.Add("Overnight");
    }

    private void SaveButton_Click(object sender, RoutedEventArgs e)
    {
      switch (PackageType.SelectedValue)
      {
        case "Base":
          package = new BasePackage();
          package.Recipient = Recipient.Text;
          package.Address = Address.Text;
          package.Weight = Int32.Parse(Weight.Text);
          package.ShipmentDate = ShipmentDate.SelectedDate ?? DateTime.Now;
          break;

        case "Advanced":
          package = new AdvancedPackage();
          package.Recipient = Recipient.Text;
          package.Address = Address.Text;
          package.Weight = Int32.Parse(Weight.Text);
          package.ShipmentDate = ShipmentDate.SelectedDate ?? DateTime.Now;
          break;

        case "Overnight":
          package = new OvernightPackage();
          package.Recipient = Recipient.Text;
          package.Address = Address.Text;
          package.Weight = Int32.Parse(Weight.Text);
          package.ShipmentDate = ShipmentDate.SelectedDate ?? DateTime.Now;
          break;
      }
      this.Close();
    }
```

```
        }
}
```

Listing 5-5: PackageForm.cs

At the end, the modal frame closes itself and control returns to the `PackageTable` class (`AddPackage_click()` method) where we repopulate the Grid with the new data:

```
private void AddPackage_Click(object sender, RoutedEventArgs e)
{
  var form = new PackageForm();
  form.ShowDialog();
  if (form.package != null)
  {
    Packages.Add(form.package);
    Ps.SaveToFile();
    PopulateGrid();
  }
}
```

Listing 5-6: MainWindow.cs

For completeness, we will include the other classes, starting with the base class `Package`:

```
using System;

namespace PackageShippingGUI
{
  public abstract class Package
  {
    private double _weight;
    public string Recipient { get; set; }
    public string Address { get; set; }
    public double Weight
    {
      get => _weight;
      set
      {
        if (value < 0)
          throw new Exception("Weight should be >= 0");
        else
          _weight = value;
      }
    }
    public DateTime ShipmentDate { get; set; }

    public Package(string recipient, string address, double weight,
      DateTime shipmentDate)
    {
      Recipient = recipient;
      Address = address;
      Weight = weight;
      ShipmentDate = shipmentDate;
    }
```

```
    public Package()
    {
      Recipient = "";
      Address = "";
      Weight = 0;
      ShipmentDate = DateTime.Now;
    }

    public abstract double CalculateCost();
    public abstract DateTime CalculateDeliveryDate();
    public override abstract string ToString();
    public abstract string Serialize();
    public abstract void Deserialize(string s);
  }
}
```

Listing 5-7: Package.cs

Here are the derived package classes:

```
using System;
using System.Text;
using System.Text.RegularExpressions;

namespace PackageShippingGUI
{
  public class BasePackage : Package
  {
    public BasePackage(string recipient, string address, double weight,
      DateTime shipmentDate) : base(recipient, address, weight, shipmentDate)
    { }

    public BasePackage() : base()
    { }

    public override double CalculateCost()
    {
      return Constants.BASE_PACKAGE_COST_FACTOR * Weight;
    }

    public override DateTime CalculateDeliveryDate()
    {
      if (Weight <= Constants.BASE_PACKAGE_MAX_WEIGHT)
        return ShipmentDate.AddDays(Constants.BASE_PACKAGE_DAYS);
      else
        return ShipmentDate.AddDays(Constants.BASE_PACKAGE_DAYS + 1);
    }

    public override string ToString()
    {
      var str = new StringBuilder();
      str.Append("\n--Base Package--");
      str.Append("\nRecipient: " + Recipient);
      str.Append("\nAddress: " + Address);
```

```
      str.Append("\nWeight: " + Weight);
      str.Append("\nShipment date:" + ShipmentDate);
      str.Append("\nExpected delivery date:" + CalculateDeliveryDate());
      str.Append("\nCost:" + CalculateCost());
      str.Append("\n--------------------");
      return str.ToString();
    }

    public override string Serialize()
    {
      var str = new StringBuilder();
      str.Append("Base Package\n");
      str.Append(Recipient + "\n");
      str.Append(Address + "\n");
      str.Append(Weight + "\n");
      str.Append(ShipmentDate + "\n");
      str.Append("--");
      return str.ToString();
    }

    public override void Deserialize(string s)
    {
      var regex = new Regex("\n");
      var lines = regex.Split(s);

      Recipient = lines[1];
      Address = lines[2];
      Weight = Double.Parse(lines[3]);
      ShipmentDate = DateTime.Parse(lines[4]);
    }
  }
}
```

Listing 5-8: BasePackage.cs

```
using System;
using System.Text;
using System.Text.RegularExpressions;

namespace PackageShippingGUI
{
  public class AdvancedPackage : Package
  {
    public AdvancedPackage(string recipient, string address, double weight,
      DateTime shipmentDate) : base(recipient, address, weight, shipmentDate)
    { }

    public AdvancedPackage() : base()
    { }

    public override double CalculateCost()
    {
      return Constants.ADVANCED_PACKAGE_COST_FACTOR * Weight
```

```csharp
                + Constants.ADVANCED_PACKAGE_COST_SUPPL;
    }

    public override DateTime CalculateDeliveryDate()
    {
        return ShipmentDate.AddDays(Constants.ADVANCED_PACKAGE_DAYS);
    }

    public override string ToString()
    {
        var str = new StringBuilder();
        str.Append("\n--Advanced Package--");
        str.Append("\nRecipient: " + Recipient);
        str.Append("\nAddress: " + Address);
        str.Append("\nWeight: " + Weight);
        str.Append("\nShipment date:" + ShipmentDate);
        str.Append("\nExpected delivery date:" + CalculateDeliveryDate());
        str.Append("\nCost:" + CalculateCost());
        str.Append("\n--------------------");
        return str.ToString();
    }

    public override string Serialize()
    {
        var str = new StringBuilder();
        str.Append("Advanced Package\n");
        str.Append(Recipient + "\n");
        str.Append(Address + "\n");
        str.Append(Weight + "\n");
        str.Append(ShipmentDate + "\n");
        str.Append("--");
        return str.ToString();
    }

    public override void Deserialize(string s)
    {
        var regex = new Regex("\n");
        var lines = regex.Split(s);

        Recipient = lines[1];
        Address = lines[2];
        Weight = Double.Parse(lines[3]);
        ShipmentDate = DateTime.Parse(lines[4]);
    }
  }
}
```

Listing 5-9: AdvancePackage.cs


```csharp
using System;
using System.Net;
using System.Text;
using System.Text.RegularExpressions;
```

```csharp
namespace PackageShippingGUI
{
  public class OvernightPackage : Package
  {
    public OvernightPackage(string recipient, string address, double weight,
      DateTime shipmentDate) : base(recipient, address, weight, shipmentDate)
    { }

    public OvernightPackage() : base()
    { }

    public override double CalculateCost()
    {
      return Constants.OVERNIGHT_PACKAGE_COST_FACTOR * Weight;
    }

    public override DateTime CalculateDeliveryDate()
    {
      return ShipmentDate.AddDays(Constants.OVERNIGHT_PACKAGE_DAYS);
    }

    public override string ToString()
    {
      var str = new StringBuilder();
      str.Append("\n--Overnight Package--");
      str.Append("\nRecipient: " + Recipient);
      str.Append("\nAddress: " + Address);
      str.Append("\nWeight: " + Weight);
      str.Append("\nShipment date:" + ShipmentDate);
      str.Append("\nExpected delivery date:" + CalculateDeliveryDate());
      str.Append("\nCost:" + CalculateCost());
      str.Append("\n--------------------");
      return str.ToString();
    }

    public override string Serialize()
    {
      var str = new StringBuilder();
      str.Append("Overnight Package\n");
      str.Append(Recipient + "\n");
      str.Append(Address + "\n");
      str.Append(Weight + "\n");
      str.Append(ShipmentDate + "\n");
      str.Append("--");
      return str.ToString();
    }

    public override void Deserialize(string s)
    {
      var regex = new Regex("\n");
      var lines = regex.Split(s);

      Recipient = lines[1];
```

```
    Address = lines[2];
    Weight = Double.Parse(lines[3]);
    ShipmentDate = DateTime.Parse(lines[4]);
  }
 }
}
```

Listing 5-10: OvernightPackage.cs

```
namespace PackageShippingGUI
{
  public class Constants
  {
    public const int BASE_PACKAGE_COST_FACTOR = 5;
    public const int BASE_PACKAGE_DAYS = 5;
    public const int BASE_PACKAGE_MAX_WEIGHT = 10;
    public const int ADVANCED_PACKAGE_COST_FACTOR = 5;
    public const int ADVANCED_PACKAGE_COST_SUPPL = 2;
    public const int ADVANCED_PACKAGE_DAYS = 2;
    public const int OVERNIGHT_PACKAGE_COST_FACTOR = 10;
    public const int OVERNIGHT_PACKAGE_DAYS = 1;
  }
}
```

Listing 5-11: Constants.cs

You can find this project in GitHub:

https://github.com/htset/csharp_oop_exercises/tree/master/PackageShippingGUI

6. Insurance

We need to create a class hierarchy that will model life and auto insurance policies of an insurance company. Both policies are characterized by the following:

- Name of the insured person
- Age of the insured person
- Coverage of the policy

In addition to that, the auto policy also depends on the vehicle age.

We should also create a method (outside of the classes) that will take an insurance policy object as input and will save it in a txt file.

In the main method, we will create a couple of insurance policies and will store them in the text file.

Proposed Solution

The base class has the following structure:

```
namespace Insurance
{
  public abstract class Insurance
  {
    public string Name { get; set; }
    public int Age { get; set; }
    public int Coverage { get; set; }

    public Insurance(string name, int age, int coverage)
    {
      Name = name;
      Age = age;
      Coverage = coverage;
    }

    public Insurance()
    {
      Name = "N/A";
      Age = 0;
      Coverage = 0;
    }

    public abstract double CalculateCost();
  }
}
```

Listing 6-1: Insurance.cs

Note that we define an abstract method, `CalculateCost()`, which makes the insurance yearly cost calculation of the policy.

We proceed with the definition of the `LifeInsurance` class:

```
using System.Text;

namespace Insurance
{
  public class LifeInsurance : Insurance
  {
    public LifeInsurance(string name, int age, int coverage)
        :base(name, age, coverage) { }

    public LifeInsurance() : base() { }

    public override double CalculateCost()
    {
      return 10 * Age + 0.001 * Coverage;
    }

    public override string ToString()
    {
      var builder = new StringBuilder();
      builder.Append("\n------Life Insurance policy------");
      builder.Append("\nName: " + Name);
      builder.Append("\nAge: " + Age);
      builder.Append("\nCoverage: " + Coverage);
      builder.Append("\nYearly cost: " + CalculateCost());

      return builder.ToString();
    }
  }
}
```

Listing 6-2: LifeInsurance.cs

Class `AutoInsurance` contains one additional parameter, the automobile age. This parameter takes part in the policy cost calculation in `CalculateCost()`:

```
using System.Text;

namespace Insurance
{
  public class AutoInsurance : Insurance
  {
    public int CarAge { get; set; }

    public AutoInsurance(String name, int age, int coverage, int carAge)
      :base(name, age, coverage)
    {
      CarAge = carAge;
    }
```

```csharp
    public AutoInsurance() : base() { }

    public override double CalculateCost()
    {
      return -Age + 0.05 * Coverage + 10 * CarAge;
    }

    public override string ToString()
    {
      var builder = new StringBuilder();
      builder.Append("\n------Auto Insurance policy------");
      builder.Append("\nName: " + Name);
      builder.Append("\nAge: " + Age);
      builder.Append("\nCoverage: " + Coverage);
      builder.Append("\nCar Age: " + CarAge);
      builder.Append("\nYearly cost: " + CalculateCost());

      return builder.ToString();
    }
  }
}
```

Listing 6-3: AutoInsurance.cs

As requested, we also need to create a method that takes an Insurance object (either of LifeInsurance or AutoInsurance type) and saves it into a text file.

We could write two separate methods that perform this task, one for each type of object. However, we can take advantage of polymorphism and *write only one method*. We put this method (as static) in Program class:

```csharp
namespace Insurance
{
  public class Program
  {
    static void SaveInsurance(Insurance insurance)
    {
      using (var writer = new StreamWriter("insurance.txt", true))
      {
        writer.WriteLine(insurance.ToString());

        //this will not compile
        //writer.WriteLine(insurance.CarAge);

        //this will work
        if (insurance.GetType().ToString().Equals("class AutoInsurance"))
          writer.WriteLine(">>>Car age: " + ((AutoInsurance)insurance).CarAge);
      }
    }
    static void Main(string[] args)
    {
      AutoInsurance i1 = new AutoInsurance("John Doe", 30, 15000, 2);
      Console.Write(i1);
      LifeInsurance i2 = new LifeInsurance("John Doe", 30, 1000000);
```

```
        Console.Write(i2);

        SaveInsurance(i1);
        SaveInsurance(i2);
      }
    }
}
```

Listing 6-4: Program.cs

This method takes a reference to Insurance as input. Through polymorphism, it calls the respective ToString() method and gets a different string each time.

Polymorphism has its limitations too. Note that we can only access the parameters and methods that are defined in the base class (Insurance). Therefore, we cannot access the CarAge property which is only defined in AutoInsurance class. If we need to do that, we have to cast the reference to a reference to AutoInsurance, like this:

```
if (insurance.GetType().ToString().Equals("class AutoInsurance"))
  writer.WriteLine(">>>Car age: " + ((AutoInsurance)insurance).CarAge);
```

You can find this project in GitHub:

https://github.com/htset/csharp_oop_exercises/tree/master/Insurance

7.Reservations

In this exercise, we will create an application that will handle reservations in apartments (in AirBnB style).

We need to manage the following information:

Apartments:

- Address
- Capacity (maximum persons)
- Price per day

Reservations:
- Name and surname of the person who made the reservation
- Start date
- Duration
- A list of the persons that will stay. For the persons, we will need to have:
  - Name and surname
  - Birth year

We will store all the information inside a MySQL database.

We will also create a console-based UI that will handle the following operations:

- Adding a new reservation
- Search for a reservation based on the surname of the person
- List all reservations

For simplicity, we will not handle the apartments in the UI. They will be inserted with SQL directly into the Apartments table. Also, we will not care about booking the same apartment more than one time, just to keep the implementation easy to follow.

Proposed Solution

We start with the definition of the database tables in SQL Server. Here is the SQL for the creation of the tables:

```
CREATE DATABASE Reservations;

CREATE TABLE Apartments (
  id int NOT NULL IDENTITY,
  address varchar(45) DEFAULT NULL,
  capacity int DEFAULT NULL,
  price decimal(10,2) DEFAULT NULL,
  PRIMARY KEY (id)
);
```

```sql
CREATE TABLE Reservations (
  id int NOT NULL IDENTITY,
  name varchar(45) DEFAULT NULL,
  surname varchar(45) DEFAULT NULL,
  start_date date DEFAULT NULL,
  duration int DEFAULT NULL,
  cost decimal(10,2) DEFAULT NULL,
  PRIMARY KEY (id)
);

CREATE TABLE Persons (
  id int NOT NULL IDENTITY,
  name varchar(45) DEFAULT NULL,
  surname varchar(45) DEFAULT NULL,
  birth_year int DEFAULT NULL,
  reservation_id int DEFAULT NULL,
  PRIMARY KEY (id)
);
```
Listing 7-1: SQL code

We can use the SQL Server Management Studio application to create the database and the corresponding tables.

Now we are ready setup-wise, so let's proceed to the code: first we define the Apartment class:

```csharp
namespace Reservations
{
  public class Apartment
  {
    public int Id { get; set; }
    public string Address { get; set; }
    public int Capacity { get; set; }
    public decimal Price { get; set; }

    public Apartment(int id, string address, int capacity, decimal price)
    {
      Id = id;
      Address = address;
      Capacity = capacity;
      Price = price;
    }

    public override string ToString()
    {
      return "--Apartment--" +
          "\nid = " + Id +
          "\naddress = " + Address +
          "\ncapacity = " + Capacity +
          "\nprice = " + Price;
    }
  }
}
```

Listing 7-2: Apartment.cs

The Reservation class is defined as follows:

```
namespace Reservations
{
  public class Reservation
  {
    public int Id { get; set; }
    public string Name { get; set; }
    public string Surname { get; set; }
    public DateTime StartDate { get; set; }
    public int Duration { get; set; }
    public decimal Cost { get; set; }
    public List<Person> Persons { get; set; }

    public Reservation(int id, string name, string surname,
                       DateTime startDate, int duration, decimal cost)
    {
      Id = id;
      Name = name;
      Surname = surname;
      StartDate = startDate;
      Duration = duration;
      Cost = cost;
      Persons = new List<Person>();
    }

    public override string ToString()
    {
      string persons = "";
      foreach(var p in Persons)
      {
        persons += p.ToString();
      }

      return "--Reservation--" +
          "\nid=" + Id +
          "\nname=" + Name +
          "\nsurname=" + Surname +
          "\nstartDate=" + StartDate +
          "\nduration=" + Duration +
          "\ncost=" + Cost +
          "\npersons=" + persons;
    }

    public void AddPerson(Person p)
    {
      Persons.Add(p);
    }
  }
}
```

Listing 7-3: Reservation.cs

The `Reservation` class contains also a list of the persons that will stay in the apartment. The `Person` class in defined below:

```
namespace Reservations
{
  public class Person
  {
    public int Id { get; set; }
    public string Name { get; set; }
    public string Surname { get; set; }
    public int BirthYear { get; set; }

    public Person(int id, string name, string surname, int birthYear)
    {
      Id = id;
      Name = name;
      Surname = surname;
      BirthYear = birthYear;
    }

    public override string ToString()
    {
      return "--Person--" +
          "\nid=" + Id +
          "\nname=" + Name +
          "\nsurname=" + Surname +
          "\nbirthYear=" + BirthYear;
    }
  }
}
```

Listing 7-4: Person.cs

The main method of the application is also very simple, as the work is delegated in the `UIService` and `PersistenceService` classes:

```
namespace Reservations
{
  public class Program
  {
    static void Main(string[] args)
    {
      var ps = new PersistenceService();
      var ui = new UIService(ps);
      ui.Menu();
    }
  }
}
```

Listing 7-5: Program.cs

Now, let's go to the interesting stuff. First the definition of the `UIService` class that handles the interaction with the user:

```
namespace Reservations
{
  public class UIService
  {
    PersistenceService Ps;

    public UIService(PersistenceService ps)
    {
      Ps = ps;
    }
    ...
  }
}
```

Listing 7-6: UIService.cs

Notice that inside the UIService class, we keep a reference to a PersistenceService object. This reference is provided in the UIService constructor.

The Menu() method contains the main loop of the interaction with the user:

```
public void Menu()
{
  int option;
  do
  {
    Console.WriteLine("Options: ");
    Console.WriteLine("1) Add reservation ");
    Console.WriteLine("2) Search reservation ");
    Console.WriteLine("3) View all reservations ");
    Console.WriteLine("0) Exit ");
    Console.Write("Enter your selection:");
    option = Convert.ToInt32(Console.ReadLine());

    switch (option)
    {
      case 1:
        AddReservation();
        break;
      case 2:
        SearchReservation();
        break;
      case 3:
        ListReservations();
        break;
      case 0:
        break;
      default:
        Console.Write("Please enter selection again:");
        break;
    }
  } while (option != 0);
}
```

Listing 7-7: UIService.cs

When the users presses 1, the `AddReservation()` method is called:

```csharp
private void AddReservation()
{
    int option;
    string name, surname;
    DateTime startDate;
    int duration;

    Console.Write("Name: ");
    name = Console.ReadLine() ?? "";

    Console.Write("Surname: ");
    surname = Console.ReadLine() ?? "";

    Console.Write("Start date (YYYY-MM-DD): ");
    DateTime.TryParse(Console.ReadLine(), out startDate);

    Console.Write("Duration: ");
    duration = Convert.ToInt32(Console.ReadLine());

    Console.WriteLine("Available apartments:");
    var apartments = Ps.GetApartments();
    int i = 1;
    foreach (var a in apartments)
    {
        Console.WriteLine("Apartment no." + (i++) + ":");
        Console.WriteLine(a);
    }
    Console.Write("(Press 0 to cancel): ");
    option = Convert.ToInt32(Console.ReadLine());

    if (option > 0 && option <= apartments.Count)
    {
        var resv = new Reservation(0, name, surname, startDate, duration,
            apartments.ElementAt(option - 1).Price);
        AddPersons(resv);
        Ps.InsertReservation(resv);
    }
}
```

Listing 7-8: UIService.cs

After entering the desired start date and duration of the reservation, the user is presented with a list of the available apartments. Normally, we would search for free apartments in those dates, but for simplicity we get all the apartments in the database.

The apartments list is retrieved with the use of the `PersistenceService` object (method `GetAvailableApartments()`). After selecting an apartment, the user is prompted to insert one by one all the persons that will stay in the apartment. This is performed with the `AddPersons()` method (a private method inside the `UIService` class):

```csharp
private void AddPersons(Reservation resv)
```

```
{
  string name, surname, selection;
  int birthYear;

  Console.WriteLine("Give the persons:");
  do
  {
    Console.Write("Name: ");
    name = Console.ReadLine() ?? "";
    Console.Write("Surname: ");
    surname = Console.ReadLine() ?? "";
    Console.Write("Birth Year: ");
    birthYear = Convert.ToInt32(Console.ReadLine());

    resv.AddPerson(new Person(0, name, surname, birthYear));

    Console.Write("Add another person? (y/n): ");
    selection = Console.ReadLine() ?? "";
  }
  while (!selection.Equals("n") && !selection.Equals("N"));
}
```

Listing 7-9: UIService.cs

Finally, there are two more methods in UIService:

```
private void SearchReservation()
{
  string surname;
  Console.Write("Enter surname (also partial): ");
  surname = Console.ReadLine() ?? "";
  var reservations = Ps.GetReservationsBySurname(surname);

  foreach (var r in reservations)
  {
    Console.WriteLine(r);
  }
}

private void ListReservations()
{
  var reservations = Ps.GetAllReservations();
  foreach (Reservation r in reservations)
  {
    Console.WriteLine(r);
  }
}
```

Listing 7-10: UIService.cs

Now, we turn to the PersistenceService class. This is the class that handles the connection with the database:

```
using System.Data;
```

```
using System.Data.SqlClient;

namespace Reservations
{
  public class PersistenceService
  {
    SqlConnection Connection;
    ...
  }
}
```
Listing 7-11: PersistenceService.cs

We put all the database functionality inside this class. Note that the other classes do not know anything about SQL Server; they just use this class. In this way, it will be easy to adapt our application to use a different database, as we will need only to write a new class like PersistenceService.

In the constructor, we create the connection with the database and a prepared statement object that will be used to send the commands to the database:

```
public PersistenceService()
{
  try
  {
    string connectionString;
    connectionString =
@"Server=localhost\SQLEXPRESS;Database=Reservations;Trusted_Connection=True;MultipleA
ctiveResultSets=true;";
    Connection = new SqlConnection(connectionString);
    Connection.Open();
  }
  catch (SqlException e)
  {
    Console.WriteLine("Could not connect to database. Exiting..");
    Console.WriteLine(e.StackTrace);
    System.Environment.Exit(1);
  }
}
```

Listing 7-12: PersistenceService.cs

All database operations are executed inside a try-catch block.

The GetApartments() method retrieves all apartments for the database:

```
public List<Apartment> GetApartments()
{
  var result = new List<Apartment>();
  try
  {
    using (var cmd = new SqlCommand())
    {
      cmd.Connection = Connection;
```

```
        cmd.CommandText = "SELECT * from Apartments";
        using (SqlDataReader reader = cmd.ExecuteReader())
        {
          while (reader.Read())
          {
            result.Add(new Apartment(reader.GetInt32(reader.GetOrdinal("id")),
                reader.GetString(reader.GetOrdinal("address")),
                reader.GetInt32(reader.GetOrdinal("capacity")),
                reader.GetInt32(reader.GetOrdinal("price")))
            );
          }
        }
      }
    }
    catch (SqlException e)
    {
      Console.Write("Database error. Exiting..");
      Console.Write(e.StackTrace);
      this.Close();
      System.Environment.Exit(1);
    }
    return result;
}
```

The GetAllReservations() method retrieves all the reservations in the database:

```
public List<Reservation> GetAllReservations()
{
  var result = new List<Reservation>();
  try
  {
    using (var cmd = new SqlCommand())
    {
      cmd.Connection = Connection;
      cmd.CommandText = "SELECT * from Reservations";
      using (SqlDataReader reader = cmd.ExecuteReader())
      {
        while (reader.Read())
        {
          var id = reader.GetInt32(reader.GetOrdinal("id"));

          Reservation resv =
            new Reservation(reader.GetInt32(reader.GetOrdinal("id")),
              reader.GetString(reader.GetOrdinal("name")),
              reader.GetString(reader.GetOrdinal("surname")),
              reader.GetDateTime(reader.GetOrdinal("start_date")),
              reader.GetInt32(reader.GetOrdinal("duration")),
              reader.GetDecimal(reader.GetOrdinal("cost")));

          using (var cmdPerson = new SqlCommand())
          {
            cmdPerson.Connection = Connection;
            cmdPerson.CommandText = "SELECT * from Persons where reservation_id=@id";
```

```
                cmdPerson.Parameters.Add("@id", SqlDbType.Int).Value = id;
                cmdPerson.Prepare();

                using (SqlDataReader readerPerson = cmdPerson.ExecuteReader())
                {
                  while (readerPerson.Read())
                  {
                    resv.AddPerson(
                      new Person(readerPerson.GetInt32(reader.GetOrdinal("id")),
                        readerPerson.GetString(readerPerson.GetOrdinal("name")),
                        readerPerson.GetString(readerPerson.GetOrdinal("surname")),
                        readerPerson.GetInt32(readerPerson.GetOrdinal("birth_year")))
                    );

                  }
                }
              }
              result.Add(resv);
            }
          }
        }
      }
      catch (SqlException e)
      {
        Console.Write("Database error. Exiting..");
        Console.Write(e.StackTrace);
        this.Close();
        System.Environment.Exit(1);
      }
      return result;
    }
```

Listing 7-14: PersistenceService.cs

The GetReservationsBySurname() method returns a list of reservations for a specific surname:

```
public List<Reservation> GetReservationsBySurname(string surname)
{
  var result = new List<Reservation>();
  try
  {
    using (var cmd = new SqlCommand())
    {
      cmd.Connection = Connection;
      cmd.CommandText = @"SELECT * from Reservations where surname like @surname";
      cmd.Parameters.Add("@surname", SqlDbType.NVarChar, 45).Value
        = "%" + surname + "%";
      cmd.Prepare();

      using (SqlDataReader reader = cmd.ExecuteReader())
      {
        while (reader.Read())
        {
```

```
        Reservation resv = new
          Reservation(reader.GetInt32(reader.GetOrdinal("id")),
            reader.GetString(reader.GetOrdinal("name")),
            reader.GetString(reader.GetOrdinal("surname")),
            reader.GetDateTime(reader.GetOrdinal("start_date")),
            reader.GetInt32(reader.GetOrdinal("duration")),
            reader.GetDecimal(reader.GetOrdinal("cost")));

        result.Add(resv);
      }
    }
  }
}
catch (SqlException e)
{
  Console.Write("Database error. Exiting..");
  Console.Write(e.StackTrace);
  this.Close();
  System.Environment.Exit(1);
}
return result;
}
```

Listing 7-15: PersistenceService.cs

We also have a method to insert a new reservation (and the corresponding persons) in the database:

```
public void InsertReservation(Reservation resv)
{
  using (var transaction = Connection.BeginTransaction())
  {
    try
    {
      using (var cmd = new SqlCommand())
      {
        cmd.Connection = Connection;
        cmd.Transaction = transaction;
        cmd.CommandText = @"insert into
          Reservations(name, surname, start_date, duration, cost)
          OUTPUT INSERTED.ID values(@name, @surname, @start_date, @duration, @cost)";
        cmd.Parameters.Add("@name", SqlDbType.NVarChar, 45).Value = resv.Name;
        cmd.Parameters.Add("@surname", SqlDbType.NVarChar, 45).Value = resv.Surname;
        cmd.Parameters.Add("@start_date", SqlDbType.DateTime).Value = resv.StartDate;
        cmd.Parameters.Add("@duration", SqlDbType.Int).Value = resv.Duration;
        cmd.Parameters.Add("@cost", SqlDbType.Decimal, 10).Value = resv.Cost;
        cmd.Parameters["@cost"].Precision = 10;
        cmd.Parameters["@cost"].Scale = 2;
        cmd.Prepare();

        var newId = (int)cmd.ExecuteScalar();

        if (newId > 0)
        {
```

```csharp
        List<Person> persons = resv.Persons;

        using (var cmdPerson = new SqlCommand())
        {
          cmdPerson.Connection = Connection;
          cmdPerson.Transaction = transaction;

          foreach (var person in persons)
          {
            cmdPerson.CommandText
              = @"insert into
                 Persons(name, surname, birth_year, reservation_id)
                 values(@name, @surname, @birth_year, @reservation_id)";
            cmdPerson.Parameters.Add("@name", SqlDbType.NVarChar, 45).Value
              = person.Name;
            cmdPerson.Parameters.Add("@surname", SqlDbType.NVarChar, 45).Value
              = person.Surname;
            cmdPerson.Parameters.Add("@birth_year", SqlDbType.Int).Value
              = person.BirthYear;
            cmdPerson.Parameters.Add("@reservation_id", SqlDbType.Int).Value
              = newId;
            cmdPerson.Prepare();
            cmdPerson.ExecuteNonQuery();
          }
        }
      }
    }
    transaction.Commit();
  }
  catch (SqlException e)
  {
    transaction.Rollback();
    Console.Write("Database error. Exiting..");
    Console.Write(e.StackTrace);
    this.Close();
    System.Environment.Exit(1);
  }
 }
}
```

Listing 7-16: PersistenceService.cs

In `InsertReservation()` we first create a new transaction, as we are going to make successive insert statements. Then we insert a new row in the `Reservations` table. The `id` field of the reservation is created automatically by the database, as we have defined it as `IDENTITY` during the creation of the table.

Upon successful insertion of the row, we get the newly generated reservation id, because we need to use it in each new `Persons` row (in the `reservation_id` field).

We perform successive inserts, one for each person, and at the end we commit our changes. In case of an exception, we can rollback the transaction and return to where we started.

Finally, we provide a `Close()` method, that closes the connection:

```csharp
private void Close()
{
  try
  {
    if (Connection != null)
    {
      Connection.Close();
      Connection.Dispose();
    }
  }
  catch (Exception e)
  {
    Console.Write("Error: Could not close connection");
    Console.Write(e.StackTrace);
  }
}
```

Listing 7-17: PersistenceService.cs

You can find this project in GitHub:

https://github.com/htset/csharp_oop_exercises/tree/master/Reservations

8. Tax declaration

In this exercise, we will create an application for the submission of property tax declarations. Our application will support three kinds of properties (Apartment, Store and Plot) with different methods for calculating the corresponding tax:

- Apartment: Tax = 1.3 * surface + 10* floor + 150
- Store: Tax = 2.5 * surface + 20* commerciality + 100
- Plot: Tax = 0.3 * surface + 100 * cultivated + 200 * withinCityLimits

The tax depends on the following parameters:

- The surface area of the property
- The floor of the apartment
- The commerciality of the store (a number between 1 and 5 that characterizes the importance of the store's road in commerce)
- Whether the plot of land is cultivated or not
- Whether the plot of land is within city limits or not

We will create a user interface that will provide users with the following options:

- Create a new tax declaration and calculate the resulting tax according to the properties declared
- Delete an existing tax declaration
- Search for declaration(-s)

Moreover, the application should provide the following statistics on the tax declarations:

- The total tax of all declarations
- The declaration with the highest tax incurred

We will create the application to be persistence agnostic. That is, we will provide the option to store the declarations in a text file and in a database.

Proposed Solution

Let's start with the definition of the Property base class:

```
namespace TaxDeclaration
{
  public abstract class Property
  {
    public int Id { get; set; }
    public int Surface { get; set; }
    public Address Address { get; set; }
```

```csharp
    public Property(int id, int surface, Address address)
    {
      Id = id;
      Surface = surface;
      Address = address;
    }

    public Property()
    {
      Id = 0;
      Surface= 0;
      Address = new Address();
    }

    public abstract double CalculateTax();
  }
}
```

Note that Property defines one abstract method (CalculateTax()). This makes it an abstract class, which means that we cannot define objects of class Property. Derived classes would have to implement this method in order to be able to be instantiated.

The Property class contains the Surface property, which is common between all types of Property. It also contains an Address object, defined below:

```csharp
using System.IO;

namespace TaxDeclaration
{
  public class Address
  {
    public string Street { get; set; }
    public string No { get; set; }
    public string Zip { get; set; }
    public string City { get; set; }

    public Address(string street, string no, string zip, string city)
    {
      Street = street;
      No = no;
      Zip = zip;
      City = city;
    }

    public Address()
    {
      Street = "N/A";
      No = "N/A";
      Zip = "N/A";
      City = "N/A";
    }
```

```
    public override string ToString()
    {
      return "Address{" +
          "street='" + Street + '\'' +
          ", number='" + No + '\'' +
          ", zip='" + Zip + '\'' +
          ", city='" + City + '\'' +
          '}';
    }
  }
}
```

Listing 8-2: Address.cs

Next, we add the Apartment class:

```
namespace TaxDeclaration
{
  public class Apartment : Property
  {
    public int Floor { get; set; }

    public Apartment(int id, int surface, Address address, int floor)
      : base(id, surface, address)
    {
      Floor = floor;
    }

    public Apartment() : base() { }

    public override string ToString()
    {
      return "Apartment{" +
          "floor=" + Floor +
          ", id=" + Id +
          ", surface=" + Surface +
          ", address=" + Address +
          '}';
    }

    public override double CalculateTax()
    {
      return (1.3 * Surface + 10 * Floor + 150);
    }
  }
}
```

Listing 8-3: Apartment.cs

The Apartment class inherits from the Property class and adds a new parameter: Floor.

Now, we add the Store class. This class adds the Commerciality property that measures how profitable is the neighborhood with regard to commerce:

```
namespace TaxDeclaration
{
  public class Store : Property
  {
    public int Commerciality;

    public Store(int id, int surface, Address address, int commerciality)
      : base(id, surface, address)
    {
      Commerciality = commerciality;
    }

    public Store() : base() { }

    public override string ToString()
    {
      return "Store{" +
          "commerciality=" + Commerciality +
          ", id=" + Id +
          ", surface=" + Surface +
          ", address=" + Address +
          '}';
    }

    public override double CalculateTax()
    {
      return (2.5 * Surface + 20 * Commerciality + 100);
    }
  }
}
```

Listing 8-4: Store.cs

The third class that subclasses Property is Plot. This class models plots of land that can be cultivated, or may be located inside a city (which makes them more profitable):

```
namespace TaxDeclaration
{
  public class Plot : Property
  {
    public bool WithinCityLimits { get; set; }
    public bool Cultivated { get; set; }

    public Plot(int id, int surface, Address address, bool withinCityLimits,
      bool cultivated) : base(id, surface, address)
    {
      this.WithinCityLimits = withinCityLimits;
      this.Cultivated = cultivated;
    }

    public Plot() : base() { }

    public override string ToString()
    {
```

```
      return "Plot{" +
          "withinCityLimits=" + WithinCityLimits +
          ", cultivated=" + Cultivated +
          ", id=" + Id +
          ", surface=" + Surface +
          ", address=" + Address +
          '}';
   }

   public override double CalculateTax()
   {
      return (0.3 * Surface + 100 * (Cultivated ? 1 : 0)
        + 200 * (WithinCityLimits ? 1 : 0));
   }
 }
}
```

Listing 8-5: Plot.cs

Now that we have defined our core classes, let's move to the services that use them. The `Main()` method is very simple:

```
namespace TaxDeclaration
{
  public class Program
  {
    static void Main(string[] args)
    {
      IPersistenceService ps = new DBService();
      //IPersistenceService ps = new FileService("td.json");
      StatisticsService ss = new StatisticsService(ps);
      UIService ui = new UIService(ps, ss);
      ui.Menu();
    }
  }
}
```

Listing 8-6: Main.cs

The important thing we do here is create one object from each of the following classes:

- `UIService`: interaction with user (console-based)
- `StatisticsService`: provision of statistics
- `IPersistenceService`: data storage

`IPersistenceService` is an *interface* that the `UIService` should use in order to handle saving, deleting and searching data from the database or a file:

```
namespace TaxDeclaration
{
  public interface IPersistenceService
  {
    void InsertTaxDeclaration(TaxDeclaration td);
```

```
        void RemoveTaxDeclaration(TaxDeclaration td);
        List<TaxDeclaration> GetTaxDeclarations(string vat, int year);
    }
}
```

Listing 8-7: IPersistenceService.cs

This interface defines three methods, to insert, delete and search for data. UIService will use those three methods to interact with data storage. UIService will be agnostic to the underlying storage; the storage can be a database of a file (or even something else). It all depends on what kind of object we decide to pass in the constructor of the UIService class (DBService or FileService). It the above snippet we have chosen to use the DBService object.

With that in mind, let's see first how UIService works:

```
namespace TaxDeclaration
{
    public class UIService
    {
        private IPersistenceService Ps;
        private StatisticsService Ss;

        ...
    }
}
```

Listing 8-8: UIService.cs

The UIService class has only two public classes, the constructor and the Menu() method:

```
public UIService(IPersistenceService ps, StatisticsService ss)
{
    Ps = ps;
    Ss = ss;
}

public void Menu()
{
    int sel;
    var td = new TaxDeclaration();
    do
    {
        Console.WriteLine("Options: ");
        Console.WriteLine("--Transactions--");
        Console.WriteLine("1: Add new Tax Declaration");
        Console.WriteLine("2: Delete Tax Declaration: ");
        Console.WriteLine("3: Find Tax Declaration: ");
        Console.WriteLine("--Statistics--");
        Console.WriteLine("11: Get total tax");
        Console.WriteLine("12: Get Tax Declaration with highest tax");
        Console.WriteLine("0: exit");

        Console.Write("Your choice: ");
        sel = Convert.ToInt32(Console.ReadLine());
```

```
  switch (sel)
  {
    case 1:
      Create();
      break;
    case 2:
      Remove();
      break;
    case 3:
      Search();
      break;
    case 11:
      Console.WriteLine("Total Tax is: " + Ss.GetTotalTax());
      break;
    case 12:
      td = Ss.GetHighestDeclaration();
      Console.WriteLine("Highest Tax Declaration is: ");
      Console.WriteLine(td);
      break;
    default:
      break;
  }
} while (sel != 0);
}
```

Listing 8-9: UIService.cs

Note how we store the references to the other objects (of type IPersistenceService and StatisticsService) in the constructor. Moreover, note the loop that runs in the Menu() method.

Next, here are the Create(), Remove() and Search() methods of the UIService class:

```
private void Create()
{
  string sel = "y";
  Console.WriteLine("Enter person details");
  var tax = EnterTaxDeclarationDetails();

  Console.WriteLine("Now enter properties: ");
  while (sel.Equals("y"))
  {
    var p = EnterProperty();
    if (p != null)
    {
      tax.AddProperty(p);
      Console.WriteLine("Property added");
    }
    else
      Console.WriteLine("No property added (user aborted)");

    Console.WriteLine("Would you like to add another property? (y/n)");
    sel = Console.ReadLine() ?? "n";
```

```csharp
    }
      Ps.InsertTaxDeclaration(tax);
      Console.WriteLine("Tax declaration added!");
  }

private void Remove()
{
  string sel;
  string search_vat;
  int submissionYear;
  Console.Write("Enter VAT number for search: ");
  search_vat = Console.ReadLine() ?? "";
  Console.Write("Enter submission year: ");
  submissionYear = Convert.ToInt32(Console.ReadLine());
  var td = Ps.GetTaxDeclarations(search_vat, submissionYear);

  if (td.Count == 1)
  {
    Console.WriteLine("Found Tax Declaration:");
    Console.WriteLine(td.ElementAt(0).ToString());
    Console.WriteLine("Delete Tax Declaration? (y/n) ");
    sel = Console.ReadLine() ?? "n";

    if (sel.Equals("y"))
    {
      Ps.RemoveTaxDeclaration(td.ElementAt(0));
      Console.WriteLine(" Tax declaration deleted");
    }
    else
    {
      Console.WriteLine(" Tax declaration NOT deleted");
    }
  }
  else
    Console.WriteLine("tax declaration not found");
}

private void Search()
{
  string search_vat;
  int submissionYear;
  Console.Write("Enter VAT number for search (press return for all VATs): ");
  search_vat = Console.ReadLine() ?? "";
  Console.Write("Enter submission year (press 0 for all years): ");
  submissionYear = Convert.ToInt32(Console.ReadLine());

  var td = Ps.GetTaxDeclarations(search_vat, submissionYear);
  Console.WriteLine("-----Tax Declarations-----");
  foreach (var tax in td)
    Console.WriteLine(tax);
}
```

Listing 8-10: UIService.cs

Those methods make use of three other methods, in order to get all the information from the user:

```
private TaxDeclaration EnterTaxDeclarationDetails()
{
  string name, surname, vat, tel;
  int year;
  Console.Write("Name: ");
  name = Console.ReadLine() ?? "";
  Console.Write("\nSurname: ");
  surname = Console.ReadLine() ?? "";
  Console.Write("\nVAT number: ");
  vat = Console.ReadLine() ?? "";
  Console.Write("\nTelephone: ");
  tel = Console.ReadLine() ?? "";
  Console.Write("\nFiscal Year: ");
  year = Convert.ToInt32(Console.ReadLine());

  return new TaxDeclaration(0, name, surname, vat, tel, year);
}

private Address EnterAddress()
{
  string street, number, zip, city;
  Console.Write("Street: ");
  street = Console.ReadLine() ?? "";
  Console.WriteLine("\nNumber: ");
  number = Console.ReadLine() ?? "";
  Console.WriteLine("\nZip code: ");
  zip = Console.ReadLine() ?? "";
  Console.WriteLine("\nCity: ");
  city = Console.ReadLine() ?? "";

  return new Address(street, number, zip, city);
}

private Property? EnterProperty()
{
  string sel, inside, cultivated;
  Address address;
  int surface, floor, commerciality;

  Console.Write("Select 1 for Apartment, 2 for Store, 3 for Plot, any other to abort: ");
  sel = Console.ReadLine() ?? "";

  switch (sel)
  {
    case "1":
      address = EnterAddress();
      Console.Write("Surface: ");
      surface = Convert.ToInt32(Console.ReadLine());

      Console.WriteLine("Floor: ");
```

```
      floor = Convert.ToInt32(Console.ReadLine());

      return new Apartment(0, surface, address, floor);
    case "2":
      address = EnterAddress();
      Console.Write("Surface: ");
      surface = Convert.ToInt32(Console.ReadLine());

      Console.Write("Commerciality: ");
      commerciality = Convert.ToInt32(Console.ReadLine());

      return new Store(0, surface, address, commerciality);
    case "3":
      address = EnterAddress();
      Console.Write("Surface: ");
      surface = Convert.ToInt32(Console.ReadLine());
      Console.Write("Inside town? ");
      inside = Console.ReadLine() ?? "n";
      Console.Write("Cultivated?");
      cultivated = Console.ReadLine() ?? "n";
      return new Plot(0, surface, address, (inside.Equals("y")) ? true : false,
        (cultivated.Equals("y")) ? true : false);
    default:
      return null;
  }
}
```

Listing 8-11: UIService.cs

The StatisticsService class provides the interface for retrieving statistics about the tax declarations:

```
namespace TaxDeclaration
{
  public class StatisticsService
  {
    IPersistenceService Ps;

    public StatisticsService(IPersistenceService ps)
    {
      Ps = ps;
    }

    public double GetTotalTax()
    {
      double totalTax = 0;
      foreach (var td in Ps.GetTaxDeclarations("", 0))
      {
        totalTax += td.CalculateTax();
      }
      return totalTax;
    }

    public TaxDeclaration? GetHighestDeclaration()
```

```
    {
        var declarations = Ps.GetTaxDeclarations("", 0);

        if (declarations.Count > 0)
        {
            var max = declarations.ElementAt(0);
            double highestTax = 0;
            foreach (var td in declarations)
            {
                if (td.CalculateTax() > highestTax)
                {
                    max = td;
                    highestTax = td.CalculateTax();
                }
            }
            return max;
        }
        else
            return null;
    }
  }
}
```

Listing 8-12: StatisticsService.cs

Note how the StatisticsService class uses the reference to the object that implements the interface defined by IPersistenceService.

Now, let's see how we can use an SQL Server database to store data on tax declarations. First we have to create the tables in the Tax database:

```
CREATE TABLE addresses (
    id int NOT NULL IDENTITY,
    street varchar(50) DEFAULT NULL,
    number varchar(50) DEFAULT NULL,
    zip varchar(50) DEFAULT NULL,
    city varchar(50) DEFAULT NULL,
    propertyId int DEFAULT NULL,
    PRIMARY KEY (id)
);

CREATE TABLE apartments (
    id int NOT NULL IDENTITY,
    surface int DEFAULT NULL,
    floor int DEFAULT NULL,
    taxDeclarationId int DEFAULT NULL,
    PRIMARY KEY (id)
);

CREATE TABLE plots (
    id int NOT NULL IDENTITY,
    surface int DEFAULT NULL,
    cultivated int DEFAULT NULL,
    withinCityLimits int DEFAULT NULL,
```

```sql
  taxDeclarationId int DEFAULT NULL,
  PRIMARY KEY (id)
);

CREATE TABLE stores (
  id int NOT NULL IDENTITY,
  surface int DEFAULT NULL,
  commerciality int DEFAULT NULL,
  taxDeclarationId int DEFAULT NULL,
  PRIMARY KEY (id)
);

CREATE TABLE taxdeclarations (
  id int NOT NULL IDENTITY,
  name varchar(50) DEFAULT NULL,
  surname varchar(50) DEFAULT NULL,
  vat varchar(20) DEFAULT NULL,
  phone varchar(20) DEFAULT NULL,
  submissionYear int DEFAULT NULL,
  PRIMARY KEY (id)
);
```

Listing 8-13: SQL code

Next, we define the DBService class that derives from IPersistenceService:

```csharp
using System.Data;
using System.Data.SqlClient;

namespace TaxDeclaration
{
  public class DBService : IPersistenceService
  {
    SqlConnection Connection;

    public DBService()
    {
      try
      {
        string connectionString;
        connectionString =
@"Server=localhost\SQLEXPRESS;Database=TaxDeclarations;Trusted_Connection=True;Multip
leActiveResultSets=true;";
        Connection = new SqlConnection(connectionString);
        Connection.Open();
      }
      catch (SqlException e)
      {
        Console.WriteLine("Could not connect to database. Exiting..");
        Console.WriteLine(e.StackTrace);
        System.Environment.Exit(1);
      }
    }
  ...
  }
```

```
}
```
Listing 8-14: DBService.cs

Note how, in the constructor, we create a new `SQLConnection` with Windows Authentication.

Method `GetTaxDeclarations()` searches the database for tax declarations with specific VAT number and submission year:

```
public List<TaxDeclaration> GetTaxDeclarations(String vat, int year)
{
  var result = new List<TaxDeclaration>();
  try
  {
    using (var cmd = new SqlCommand())
    {
      cmd.Connection = Connection;

      if (vat != "")
      {
        if (year != 0)
        {
          cmd.CommandText = @"SELECT * from TaxDeclarations
            WHERE vat = @vat and submissionYear = @submissionYear ";
          cmd.Parameters.Add("@vat", SqlDbType.NVarChar, 20).Value = vat;
          cmd.Parameters.Add("@submissionYear", SqlDbType.Int).Value = year;
        }
        else
        {
          cmd.CommandText = @"SELECT * from TaxDeclarations WHERE vat = @vat ";
          cmd.Parameters.Add("@vat", SqlDbType.NVarChar, 20).Value = vat;
        }
      }
      else
      {
        if (year != 0)
        {
          cmd.CommandText = @"SELECT * from TaxDeclarations
            WHERE submissionYear = @submissionYear ";
          cmd.Parameters.Add("@submissionYear", SqlDbType.Int).Value = year;
        }
        else
        {
          cmd.CommandText = @"SELECT * from TaxDeclarations ";
        }
      }

      cmd.Prepare();

      using (SqlDataReader reader = cmd.ExecuteReader())
      {
        while (reader.Read())
        {
          TaxDeclaration td = new TaxDeclaration(
            reader.GetInt32(reader.GetOrdinal("id")),
```

```csharp
        reader.GetString(reader.GetOrdinal("name")),
        reader.GetString(reader.GetOrdinal("surname")),
        reader.GetString(reader.GetOrdinal("vat")),
        reader.GetString(reader.GetOrdinal("phone")),
        reader.GetInt32(reader.GetOrdinal("submissionYear"))
    );

    using (var cmdProperty = new SqlCommand())
    {
        cmdProperty.Connection = Connection;
        cmdProperty.CommandText = @"SELECT * from Apartments
          WHERE taxDeclarationId = @taxDeclarationId";
        cmdProperty.Parameters.Add("@taxDeclarationId", SqlDbType.Int).Value
          = reader.GetInt32(reader.GetOrdinal("id"));

        using (SqlDataReader readerProperty = cmdProperty.ExecuteReader())
        {
            while (readerProperty.Read())
            {
                using (var cmdAddress = new SqlCommand())
                {
                    cmdAddress.Connection = Connection;
                    cmdAddress.CommandText = @"SELECT * from Addresses
                      where propertyId = @propertyId";
                    cmdAddress.Parameters.Add("@propertyId", SqlDbType.Int).Value
                      = readerProperty.GetInt32(readerProperty.GetOrdinal("id"));

                    using (SqlDataReader readerAddress = cmdAddress.ExecuteReader())
                    {
                        while (readerProperty.Read())
                        {
                            Address addr = new Address(
                              readerAddress.GetString(readerAddress.GetOrdinal("street")),
                              readerAddress.GetString(readerAddress.GetOrdinal("number")),
                              readerAddress.GetString(readerAddress.GetOrdinal("zip")),
                              readerAddress.GetString(readerAddress.GetOrdinal("city"))
                            );

                            Apartment ap = new Apartment(
                              readerProperty.GetInt32(readerProperty.GetOrdinal("id")),
                              readerProperty
                                .GetInt32(readerProperty.GetOrdinal("surface")),
                              addr,
                              readerProperty.GetInt32(readerProperty.GetOrdinal("floor"))
                            );

                            td.AddProperty(ap);
                        }
                    }
                }
            }
        }
    }
}
```

```csharp
using (var cmdProperty = new SqlCommand())
{
  cmdProperty.Connection = Connection;
  cmdProperty.CommandText = @"SELECT * from Stores
    WHERE taxDeclarationId = @taxDeclarationId";
  cmdProperty.Parameters.Add("@taxDeclarationId", SqlDbType.Int).Value
    = reader.GetInt32(reader.GetOrdinal("id"));

  using (SqlDataReader readerProperty = cmdProperty.ExecuteReader())
  {
    while (readerProperty.Read())
    {
      using (var cmdAddress = new SqlCommand())
      {
        cmdAddress.Connection = Connection;
        cmdAddress.CommandText = @"SELECT * from Addresses
          WHERE propertyId = @propertyId";
        cmdAddress.Parameters.Add("@propertyId", SqlDbType.Int).Value
          = readerProperty.GetInt32(reader.GetOrdinal("id"));

        using (SqlDataReader readerAddress = cmdAddress.ExecuteReader())
        {
          while (readerProperty.Read())
          {
            Address addr = new Address(
              readerAddress.GetString(readerAddress.GetOrdinal("street")),
              readerAddress.GetString(readerAddress.GetOrdinal("number")),
              readerAddress.GetString(readerAddress.GetOrdinal("zip")),
              readerAddress.GetString(readerAddress.GetOrdinal("city"))
            );

            Store st = new Store(
              readerProperty.GetInt32(readerProperty.GetOrdinal("id")),
              readerProperty
                .GetInt32(readerProperty.GetOrdinal("surface")),
              addr,
              readerProperty
                .GetInt32(readerProperty.GetOrdinal("commerciality"))
            );

            td.AddProperty(st);
          }
        }
      }
    }
  }
}

using (var cmdProperty = new SqlCommand())
{
  cmdProperty.Connection = Connection;
  cmdProperty.CommandText = @"SELECT * from Plots
    WHERE taxDeclarationId = @taxDeclarationId";
  cmdProperty.Parameters.Add("@taxDeclarationId", SqlDbType.Int).Value
```

```csharp
            = reader.GetInt32(reader.GetOrdinal("id"));

        using (SqlDataReader readerProperty = cmdProperty.ExecuteReader())
        {
          while (readerProperty.Read())
          {
            using (var cmdAddress = new SqlCommand())
            {
              cmdAddress.Connection = Connection;
              cmdAddress.CommandText = @"SELECT * from Addresses
                WHERE propertyId = @propertyId";
              cmdAddress.Parameters.Add("@propertyId", SqlDbType.Int).Value
                = readerProperty.GetInt32(reader.GetOrdinal("id"));

              using (SqlDataReader readerAddress = cmdAddress.ExecuteReader())
              {
                while (readerProperty.Read())
                {
                  Address addr = new Address(
                    readerAddress.GetString(readerAddress.GetOrdinal("street")),
                    readerAddress.GetString(readerAddress.GetOrdinal("number")),
                    readerAddress.GetString(readerAddress.GetOrdinal("zip")),
                    readerAddress.GetString(readerAddress.GetOrdinal("city"))
                  );

                  Plot pl = new Plot(
                    readerProperty.GetInt32(readerProperty.GetOrdinal("id")),
                    readerProperty
                      .GetInt32(readerProperty.GetOrdinal("surface")),
                    addr,
                    readerProperty
                      .GetBoolean(readerProperty.GetOrdinal("cultivated")),
                    ReaderProperty
                      .GetBoolean(readerProperty.GetOrdinal("withinCityLimits"))
                  );
                  td.AddProperty(pl);
                }
              }
            }
          }
        }
        result.Add(td);
      }
    }
  }
}
catch (SqlException e)
{
  Console.Write("Database error. Exiting..");
  Console.Write(e.StackTrace);
  this.Close();
  System.Environment.Exit(1);
}
```

```
    return result;
  }
```

Listing 8-15: DBService.cs

Method `InsertTaxDeclaration()` inserts a new declaration in the database:

```csharp
public void InsertTaxDeclaration(TaxDeclaration td)
{
  using (var transaction = Connection.BeginTransaction())
  {
    try
    {
      using (var cmd = new SqlCommand())
      {
        cmd.Connection = Connection;
        cmd.Transaction = transaction;
        cmd.CommandText
          = @"insert into TaxDeclarations(name, surname, vat, phone, submissionYear)
          OUTPUT INSERTED.ID values(@name, @surname, @vat, @phone, @submissionYear)";
        cmd.Parameters.Add("@name", SqlDbType.NVarChar, 50).Value
          = td.Name;
        cmd.Parameters.Add("@surname", SqlDbType.NVarChar, 50).Value
          = td.Surname;
        cmd.Parameters.Add("@vat", SqlDbType.NVarChar, 20).Value
          = td.Vat;
        cmd.Parameters.Add("@phone", SqlDbType.NVarChar, 20).Value
          = td.Phone;
        cmd.Parameters.Add("@submissionYear", SqlDbType.Int).Value
          = td.SubmissionYear;
        cmd.Prepare();

        var newId = (int)cmd.ExecuteScalar();

        if (newId > 0)
        {
          var properties = td.Properties;

          using (var cmdProperty = new SqlCommand())
          {
            cmdProperty.Connection = Connection;
            cmdProperty.Transaction = transaction;

            foreach (Property p in properties)
            {
              if (p is Apartment)
              {
                Apartment temp = (Apartment)p;

                cmdProperty.CommandText
                  = @"insert into Apartments(surface, floor, taxDeclarationId)
                  OUTPUT INSERTED.ID values(@surface, @floor, @taxDeclarationId)";
                cmdProperty.Parameters.Add("@surface", SqlDbType.Int).Value
                  = temp.Surface;
                cmdProperty.Parameters.Add("@floor", SqlDbType.Int).Value
```

```csharp
        = temp.Floor;
    cmdProperty.Parameters.Add("@taxDeclarationId", SqlDbType.Int).Value
        = newId;
    cmdProperty.Prepare();

    var newPropertyId = (int)cmdProperty.ExecuteScalar();

    cmdProperty.CommandText
        = @"insert into Addresses(street, number, zip, city, propertyId)
        values(@street, @number, @zip, @city, @propertyId)";
    cmdProperty.Parameters.Add("@street", SqlDbType.NVarChar, 50).Value
        = temp.Address.Street;
    cmdProperty.Parameters.Add("@number", SqlDbType.NVarChar, 50).Value
        = temp.Address.No;
    cmdProperty.Parameters.Add("@zip", SqlDbType.NVarChar, 50).Value
        = temp.Address.Zip;
    cmdProperty.Parameters.Add("@city", SqlDbType.NVarChar, 50).Value
        = temp.Address.City;
    cmdProperty.Parameters.Add("@propertyId", SqlDbType.Int).Value
        = newPropertyId;
    cmdProperty.Prepare();
    cmdProperty.ExecuteNonQuery();
}
else if (p is Store)
{
    Store temp = (Store)p;

    cmdProperty.CommandText
        = @"insert into Stores(surface, commerciality, taxDeclarationId)
        OUTPUT INSERTED.ID values(@surface, @commerciality,
        @taxDeclarationId)";
    cmdProperty.Parameters.Add("@surface", SqlDbType.Int).Value
        = temp.Surface;
    cmdProperty.Parameters.Add("@commerciality", SqlDbType.Int).Value
        = temp.Commerciality;
    cmdProperty.Parameters.Add("@taxDeclarationId", SqlDbType.Int).Value
        = newId;
    cmdProperty.Prepare();

    var newPropertyId = (int)cmdProperty.ExecuteScalar();

    cmdProperty.CommandText
        = @"insert into Addresses(street, number, zip, city, propertyId)
        values(@street, @number, @zip, @city, @propertyId)";
    cmdProperty.Parameters.Add("@street", SqlDbType.NVarChar, 50).Value
        = temp.Address.Street;
    cmdProperty.Parameters.Add("@number", SqlDbType.NVarChar, 50).Value
        = temp.Address.No;
    cmdProperty.Parameters.Add("@zip", SqlDbType.NVarChar, 50).Value
        = temp.Address.Zip;
    cmdProperty.Parameters.Add("@city", SqlDbType.NVarChar, 50).Value
        = temp.Address.City;
    cmdProperty.Parameters.Add("@propertyId", SqlDbType.Int).Value
        = newPropertyId;
```

```csharp
                    cmdProperty.Prepare();
                    cmdProperty.ExecuteNonQuery();
                }
                if (p is Plot)
                {
                    Plot temp = (Plot)p;

                    cmdProperty.CommandText
                        = @"insert into Plots(surface, cultivated, withinCityLimits,
                        taxDeclarationId) OUTPUT INSERTED.ID
                        values(@surface, @cultivated, @withinCityLimits,
                        @taxDeclarationId)";
                    cmdProperty.Parameters.Add("@surface", SqlDbType.Int).Value
                        = temp.Surface;
                    cmdProperty.Parameters.Add("@cultivated", SqlDbType.Bit).Value
                        = temp.Cultivated;
                    cmdProperty.Parameters.Add("@withinCityLimits", SqlDbType.Bit).Value
                        = temp.WithinCityLimits;
                    cmdProperty.Parameters.Add("@taxDeclarationId", SqlDbType.Int).Value
                        = newId;
                    cmdProperty.Prepare();

                    var newPropertyId = (int)cmdProperty.ExecuteScalar();

                    cmdProperty.CommandText
                        = @"insert into Addresses(street, number, zip, city, propertyId)
                        values(@street, @number, @zip, @city, @propertyId)";
                    cmdProperty.Parameters.Add("@street", SqlDbType.NVarChar, 50).Value
                        = temp.Address.Street;
                    cmdProperty.Parameters.Add("@number", SqlDbType.NVarChar, 50).Value
                        = temp.Address.No;
                    cmdProperty.Parameters.Add("@zip", SqlDbType.NVarChar, 50).Value
                        = temp.Address.Zip;
                    cmdProperty.Parameters.Add("@city", SqlDbType.NVarChar, 50).Value
                        = temp.Address.City;
                    cmdProperty.Parameters.Add("@propertyId", SqlDbType.Int).Value
                        = newPropertyId;
                    cmdProperty.Prepare();
                    cmdProperty.ExecuteNonQuery();
                }
            }
        }
    }
}
transaction.Commit();
}
catch (SqlException e)
{
    transaction.Rollback();
    Console.Write("Database error. Exiting..");
    Console.Write(e.StackTrace);
    this.Close();
    System.Environment.Exit(1);
}
```

```
    }
}
```

Listing 8-16: DBService.cs

Next, `RemoveTaxDeclaration()` method, deletes a declaration from the database (and all the Properties and Addresses that are connected to it):

```
public void RemoveTaxDeclaration(TaxDeclaration td)
{
  using (var transaction = Connection.BeginTransaction())
  {
    try
    {
      using (var cmd = new SqlCommand())
      {
        cmd.Connection = Connection;
        cmd.Transaction = transaction;

        cmd.CommandText = @"delete from Addresses
          where propertyId in (select id from Apartments
            where taxDeclarationId = @taxDeclarationId)";
        cmd.Parameters.Add("@taxDeclarationId", SqlDbType.Int).Value
          = td.Id;
        cmd.Prepare();
        cmd.ExecuteNonQuery();

        cmd.CommandText = @"delete from Apartments
          where taxDeclarationId = @taxDeclarationId";
        cmd.Parameters.Add("@taxDeclarationId", SqlDbType.Int).Value
          = td.Id;
        cmd.Prepare();
        cmd.ExecuteNonQuery();

        cmd.CommandText = @"delete from Addresses
          where propertyId in (select id from Stores
            where taxDeclarationId = @taxDeclarationId)";
        cmd.Parameters.Add("@taxDeclarationId", SqlDbType.Int).Value
          = td.Id;
        cmd.Prepare();
        cmd.ExecuteNonQuery();

        cmd.CommandText = @"delete from Stores
          where taxDeclarationId = @taxDeclarationId";
        cmd.Parameters.Add("@taxDeclarationId", SqlDbType.Int).Value
          = td.Id;
        cmd.Prepare();
        cmd.ExecuteNonQuery();

        cmd.CommandText = @"delete from Addresses
          where propertyId in (select id from Plots
            where taxDeclarationId = @taxDeclarationId)";
        cmd.Parameters.Add("@taxDeclarationId", SqlDbType.Int).Value
          = td.Id;
```

```
    cmd.Prepare();
    cmd.ExecuteNonQuery();

    cmd.CommandText = @"delete from Plots
      where taxDeclarationId = @taxDeclarationId";
    cmd.Parameters.Add("@taxDeclarationId", SqlDbType.Int).Value
      = td.Id;
    cmd.Prepare();
    cmd.ExecuteNonQuery();

    cmd.CommandText = @"delete from TaxDeclarations
      where id = @taxDeclarationId";
    cmd.Parameters.Add("@taxDeclarationId", SqlDbType.Int).Value
      = td.Id;
    cmd.Prepare();
    cmd.ExecuteNonQuery();
    }
    transaction.Commit();
  }
  catch (SqlException e)
  {
    transaction.Rollback();
    Console.Write("Database error. Exiting..");
    Console.Write(e.StackTrace);
    this.Close();
    System.Environment.Exit(1);
  }
 }
}
```

Listing 8-17: DBService.cs

Finally, the Close() method:

```
private void Close()
{
  try
  {
    if (Connection != null)
    {
      Connection.Close();
    }
  }
  catch (SqlException e)
  {
    Console.Write("Database error. Exiting..");
    Console.Write(e.StackTrace);
    System.Environment.Exit(1);
  }
}
```

Listing 8-18: DBService.cs

Next, we define the `FileService` class, which is used to store data in a text file:

```
using System.Text.Json;

namespace TaxDeclaration
{
  public class FileService : IPersistenceService
  {
    List<TaxDeclaration> Declarations;
    string Filename;
    private readonly JsonSerializerOptions Options
        = new()
        {
          Converters = { new PropertyConverter() },
          WriteIndented = true,
        };

    public FileService(string filename)
    {
      Filename = filename;
      Declarations = new List<TaxDeclaration>();
      LoadFromFile();
    }
    ...
  }
}
```

Listing 8-19: FileService.cs

Note that in the constructor of the `FileService` class we open a text file and we load all the data it contains.

The `LoadFromFile()` method is private inside the class and loads the data from the text file into a list of `TaxDeclaration` objects:

```
public void LoadFromFile()
{
  Declarations.Clear();

  if (!File.Exists(Filename))
  {
    var newFile = File.Create(Filename);
    newFile.Close();
  }

  string json = File.ReadAllText(Filename);
  if (json != null && json.Length > 0)
    Declarations
        = (JsonSerializer.Deserialize<TaxDeclaration[]>(json, Options)).ToList();
}
```

Listing 8-20: FileService.cs

In `FileService`, we store the data in JSON format by using the System.Text.Json library. System.Text.Json enables us to transform an entire array of objects in JSON format in a simple method call. Note how the `JsonSerializer` object can parse a JSON array into an `TaxDeclaration` array in one go (through method `Deserialize()`).

System.Text.Json also enables us to transform an array of `TaxDeclaration` objects into a JSON array. We use this in `SaveToFile()` method:

```
private void SaveToFile()
{
  using (StreamWriter writer = new StreamWriter(Filename))
  {
    writer.Write(JsonSerializer
      .Serialize<TaxDeclaration[]>(Declarations.ToArray(), Options));
  }
}
```

Listing 8-21: FileService.cs

When there is a change in the data, for example, when we create a new tax declaration, or delete an existing one, we save all the `TaxDeclaration` objects into the file (we overwrite the existing data in the file). As we pointed out in a previous exercise, it is not possible to insert or delete an entry in the middle of a text file, so we have to create a new one from scratch.

While SystemText.Json can easily parse objects as well as simple lists of objects, it needs our help when polymorphic objects are used. For instance, when a property object is read from a JSON string, the library cannot know whether it is an `Apartment`, `Store` or `Plot` object. For this to work, we create a new Class, `PropertyConverter` that will take care of the serialization and the deserialization of the property objects:

```
using System.Text.Json.Serialization;
using System.Text.Json;

namespace TaxDeclaration
{
  public class PropertyConverter : JsonConverter<Property>
  {
    public override bool CanConvert(Type typeToConvert) =>
        typeof(Property).IsAssignableFrom(typeToConvert);

    public override Property Read(ref Utf8JsonReader reader,
        Type typeToConvert, JsonSerializerOptions options)
    {
      if (reader.TokenType != JsonTokenType.StartObject)
        throw new JsonException();
      reader.Read();
      if (reader.TokenType != JsonTokenType.PropertyName)
        throw new JsonException();
      string? propertyName = reader.GetString();
      if (propertyName != "PropertyType")
        throw new JsonException();
```

```csharp
reader.Read();
if (reader.TokenType != JsonTokenType.String)
  throw new JsonException();
var propertyType = reader.GetString();
Property property;
switch (propertyType)
{
  case "Apartment":
    property = new Apartment();
    break;
  case "Store":
    property = new Store();
    break;
  case "Plot":
    property = new Plot();
    break;
  default:
    throw new JsonException();
};

while (reader.Read())
{
  if (reader.TokenType == JsonTokenType.EndObject)
    return property;
  if (reader.TokenType == JsonTokenType.PropertyName)
  {
    propertyName = reader.GetString();
    reader.Read();
    switch (propertyName)
    {
      case "Id":
        property.Id = reader.GetInt32();
        break;
      case "Surface":
        property.Surface = reader.GetInt32();
        break;
      case "Floor":
        int floor = reader.GetInt32();
        if (property is Apartment)
          ((Apartment)property).Floor = floor;
        else
          throw new JsonException();
        break;
      case "Commerciality":
        int commerciality = reader.GetInt32();
        if (property is Store)
          ((Store)property).Commerciality = commerciality;
        else
          throw new JsonException();
        break;
      case "WithinCityLimits":
        bool withinCityLimits = reader.GetBoolean();
        if (property is Plot)
          ((Plot)property).WithinCityLimits = withinCityLimits;
```

```csharp
              else
                throw new JsonException();
              break;
          case "Cultivated":
              bool cultivated = reader.GetBoolean();
              if (property is Plot)
                ((Plot)property).Cultivated = cultivated;
              else
                throw new JsonException();
              break;
          case "Address":
              if (reader.TokenType == JsonTokenType.StartObject)
              {
                Address address = new Address();
                while (reader.Read())
                {
                  if (reader.TokenType == JsonTokenType.EndObject)
                    break;
                  if (reader.TokenType == JsonTokenType.PropertyName)
                  {
                    propertyName = reader.GetString();
                    reader.Read();
                    switch (propertyName)
                    {
                      case "Street":
                        address.Street = reader.GetString() ?? "";
                        break;
                      case "No":
                        address.No = reader.GetString() ?? "";
                        break;
                      case "Zip":
                        address.Zip = reader.GetString() ?? "";
                        break;
                      case "City":
                        address.City = reader.GetString() ?? "";
                        break;
                    }
                  }
                }
                property.Address = address;
              }
              break;
        }
      }
  }
  throw new JsonException();
}

public override void Write(Utf8JsonWriter writer,
    Property property, JsonSerializerOptions options)
{
  writer.WriteStartObject();
  if (property is Apartment apartment)
  {
```

```
        writer.WriteString("PropertyType", "Apartment");
        writer.WriteNumber("Surface", apartment.Surface);
        writer.WriteNumber("Floor", apartment.Floor);
        writer.WriteStartObject("Address");
        writer.WriteString("Street", apartment.Address.Street);
        writer.WriteString("No", apartment.Address.No);
        writer.WriteString("Zip", apartment.Address.Zip);
        writer.WriteString("City", apartment.Address.City);
        writer.WriteEndObject();
      }
      else if (property is Store store)
      {
        writer.WriteString("PropertyType", "Store");
        writer.WriteNumber("Surface", store.Surface);
        writer.WriteNumber("Commerciality", store.Commerciality);
        writer.WriteStartObject("Address");
        writer.WriteString("Street", store.Address.Street);
        writer.WriteString("No", store.Address.No);
        writer.WriteString("Zip", store.Address.Zip);
        writer.WriteString("City", store.Address.City);
        writer.WriteEndObject();
      }
      else if (property is Plot plot)
      {
        writer.WriteString("PropertyType", "Plot");
        writer.WriteNumber("Surface", plot.Surface);
        writer.WriteBoolean("WithinCityLimits", plot.WithinCityLimits);
        writer.WriteBoolean("Cultivated", plot.Cultivated);
        writer.WriteStartObject("Address");
        writer.WriteString("Street", plot.Address.Street);
        writer.WriteString("No", plot.Address.No);
        writer.WriteString("Zip", plot.Address.Zip);
        writer.WriteString("City", plot.Address.City);
        writer.WriteEndObject();
      }
      writer.WriteEndObject();
    }
  }
}
```

Listing 8-22: PropertyConverter.cs

The two most important methods are Read() and Write(). The former reads the JSON representation and transforms it to the object itself. The latter creates the JSON string from the object. We see that PropertyConverter adds the actual class name in the Property object, in the resulting JSON string:

```
{
  "PropertyType": "Apartment",
  "Surface": 5,
  "Floor": 3,
  "Address": {
    "Street": "f",
    "No": "f",
```

```
    "Zip": "f",
    "City": "f"
  }
}
```
Listing 8-23: JSON text

When the JSON string is parsed by the System.Text.Json library, the PropertyType property is used to find out what this object is about.

Let's see how the IPersistenceService interface implemented here. First the GetTaxDeclarations() method:

```csharp
public List<TaxDeclaration> GetTaxDeclarations(string vat, int submissionYear)
{
  if (vat.Trim().Equals("") && submissionYear == 0)
    return Declarations;

  var ret = new List<TaxDeclaration>();
  foreach (var td in Declarations)
  {
    if (!vat.Equals(""))
    {
      if (submissionYear != 0)
      {
        if (td.Vat.Equals(vat) && td.SubmissionYear == submissionYear)
          ret.Add(td);
      }
      else
      {
        if (td.Vat.Equals(vat))
          ret.Add(td);
      }
    }
    else
    {
      if (submissionYear != 0)
      {
        if (td.SubmissionYear == submissionYear)
          ret.Add(td);
      }
    }
  }
  return ret;
}
```

Listing 8-24: FileService.cs

Next, the InsertTaxDeclaration() method:

```csharp
public void InsertTaxDeclaration(TaxDeclaration td)
{
  Declarations.Add(td);
  SaveToFile();
}
```

Listing 8-25: FileService.cs

Finally, here is the RemoveTaxDeclaration() method:

```
public void RemoveTaxDeclaration(TaxDeclaration declaration)
{
  foreach (var td in Declarations)
  {
    if (td.Vat.Equals(declaration.Vat)
      && td.SubmissionYear == declaration.SubmissionYear)
    {
      Declarations.Remove(td);
      break;
    }
  }
  SaveToFile();
}
```

Listing 8-26: FileService.cs

Finally, one note about the id parameters of the TaxDeclaration and the Property classes. Since we are using databases, we need identification fields in the tables, in order to make the connections between the schema's tables. Those id values are defined as IDENTITY and are assigned by the database. Therefore, when we create a new object (e.g. of type Apartment) we give an initial value of zero to the id field.

When we use files for data storage, we ignore this parameter altogether. That is, we do not store it in the file and we keep a zero value in all object ids.

You can find this project in GitHub:

https://github.com/htset/csharp_oop_exercises/tree/master/TaxDeclaration

9. PacMan game

In this exercise we will create a simplified PacMan game.

Proposed Solution

PacMan and the Ghosts possess similar characteristics: Most important, their position in the maze. Moreover, they both need to have access to the maze so that they can find out where they can move to.

With this in mind, we define a base class called Entity:

```
namespace Pacman
{
  public enum EntityType
  {
    Pacman, Ghost
  }

  public abstract class Entity
  {
    public int x;
    public int y;
    public Direction direction;
    public EntityType type;
    public Game game;

    public void Move(int newX, int newY)
    {
      game.map[newX, newY].entity = game.map[x, y].entity;
      game.map[x, y].entity = null;
      x = newX;
      y = newY;
    }

    public abstract void Play();
  }
}
```

Listing 9-1: Entity.cs

In this class, we define the position (parameters x and y), the direction the entity is moving to, its type (PacMan or Ghost) and a reference to the Game object. The Entity class also defines one method called Move() that is used to move an entity inside the map.

Furthermore, it defines one abstract method that will be implemented in the derived classes (PacMan and Ghost). The Play() method is used to calculate the next position of the entity.

Now, let's see how the maze map is organized. The map consists of Block objects:

```
namespace Pacman
{
  public enum BlockType
  {
    Wall, Point, Empty
  }

  public class Block
  {
    public BlockType type { get; set; }
    public Entity? entity { get; set; }
  }
}
```

Listing 9-2: Block.cs

Each `Block` can be of specific `BlockType`:

- A wall
- A space with a point
- An empty space

Entities can move to spaces, either empty or with points. When an entity moves to a block, then the `entity` reference inside the Block object will be set to point to the entity object.

Each `Entity` can move to a specific `Direction`:

```
public enum Direction
{
  Up, Right, Down, Left
}
```

Listing 9-3: Game.cs

We also define a `Pair` class that will be handy with handling positions in the maze. The implementation of the `Pair` class is as follows:

```
namespace Pacman
{
  public class Pair
  {
    public int x { get; set; }
    public int y { get; set; }

    public Pair(int x, int y)
    {
      this.x = x;
      this.y = y;
    }

    public Pair()
    {
      this.x = 0;
```

```
        this.y = 0;
    }
  }
}
```

Listing 9-4: Pair.cs

Now, let's see the heart of the program, the Game class:

```
using System;
using System.Windows.Input;

namespace Pacman
{
  public enum Direction
  {
    Up, Right, Down, Left
  }

  public class Game
  {
    public Block[,] map { get; set; }
    public int sizeX = 32;
    public int sizeY = 28;
    public bool gameActive = true;
    public Pair pacmanLocation;
    public int pointsLeft;
    public Entity[] player;
...
  }
}
```

Listing 9-5: Game.cs

During construction of the Game object, we parse an array of strings that make up a text representation of the maze. We also keep track of the remaining points in the game (variable pointsLeft). Finally, we create the game entities and we place them at their initial positions in the maze:

```
public Game()
{
  map = new Block[32, 28];
  player = new Entity[4];

  pointsLeft = 0;
  for (int i = 0; i < 32; i++)
  {
    string line = Chart.chart[i];
    for (int j = 0; j < 28; j++)
    {
      map[i, j] = new Block();
      map[i, j].entity = null;

      if (line[j] == '.')
      {
```

```
      map[i, j].type = BlockType.Point;
      pointsLeft++;
    }
    else if (line[j] == '*')
      map[i, j].type = BlockType.Wall;
    if (line[j] == ' ')
      map[i, j].type = BlockType.Empty;
    }
  }

  player[0] = new PacMan(this, 23, 13);
  this.map[23, 13].entity = player[0];
  this.pacmanLocation = new Pair(23, 13);

  player[1] = new Ghost(this, 5, 5);
  this.map[5, 5].entity = player[1];

  player[2] = new Ghost(this, 5, 20);
  this.map[5, 20].entity = player[2];

  player[3] = new Ghost(this, 8, 5);
  this.map[8, 5].entity = player[3];
}
```

Listing 9-6: Game.cs

Note how the newly created entities are placed in the map. This means that we have a bidirectional relationship between the map and the entities, as each object has a reference to the other.

Here is the string array used to initialize the game map:

```
public class Chart
{
  public static string[] chart =
    {
      "*************************",
      "*.............**...........*",
      "*.****.*****.**.*****.****.*",
      "*.****.*****.**.*****.****.*",
      "*.****.*****.**.*****.****.*",
      "*..........................*",
      "*.****.**.*******.**.****.*",
      "*.****.**.*******.**.****.*",
      "*......**....**....**......*",
      "******.*****.**.*****.******",
      "******.*****.**.*****.******",
      "******.**          **.******",
      "******.**.********.**.******",
      "******.**.********.**.******",
      "*         ********         *",
      "******.**.********.**.******",
      "******.**.********.**.******",
      "******.**          **.******",
```

```
  "****** ** ******** ** ******",
  "****** ** ******** ** ******",
  "*.............**............*",
  "*.****.*****.**.*****.****.*",
  "*.****.*****.**.*****.****.*",
  "*...**............**...*",
  "***.**.**.********.**.**.***",
  "***.**.**.********.**.**.***",
  "***.**.**.********.**.**.***",
  "*......**....**....**......*",
  "*.*********.**.*********.*",
  "*.*********.**.*********.*",
  "*.......................*",
  "***************************"
};
}
```

Listing 9-7: Chart.cs

The asterisks denote a wall, while the dots represent spaces with points. Finally, there are some empty spaces denoted with the space symbol.

The `KeyPressed()` method gets the key code that was pressed and changes the direction of PacMan:

```
public void KeyPressed(KeyEventArgs keyEvent)
{
  Console.Write("Key pressed: " + keyEvent.Key);

  if (keyEvent.Key == Key.Up)
    player[0].direction = Direction.Up;
  if (keyEvent.Key == Key.Right)
    player[0].direction = Direction.Right;
  if (keyEvent.Key == Key.Down)
    player[0].direction = Direction.Down;
  if (keyEvent.Key == Key.Left)
    player[0].direction = Direction.Left;
}
```

Listing 9-8: Game.cs

We conclude the `Game` class definition with one more method:

```
public void PlayRound()
{
  for (int i = 0; i < 4; i++)
    player[i].Play();
}
```

Listing 9-9: Game.cs

This method is called during every loop and carries out the calculation of the entities' moves.

Speaking about the loop, let's see its implementation in the `MainWindow` file:

```xml
<Window x:Class="Pacman.MainWindow"
        xmlns="http://schemas.microsoft.com/winfx/2006/xaml/presentation"
        xmlns:x="http://schemas.microsoft.com/winfx/2006/xaml"
        xmlns:d="http://schemas.microsoft.com/expression/blend/2008"
        xmlns:mc="http://schemas.openxmlformats.org/markup-compatibility/2006"
        xmlns:local="clr-namespace:Pacman"
        mc:Ignorable="d"
        Title="MainWindow" Height="612" Width="793">
    <Grid>
        <Canvas x:Name="canvas"/>
    </Grid>
</Window>
```

Listing 9-10 MainWindow.xaml

The `MainWindow` class contains a `Canvas` object that we will use to paint the game maze.

Here is part of the code behind the window:

```csharp
using System;
using System.Windows;
using System.Windows.Controls;
using System.Windows.Input;
using System.Windows.Media;
using System.Windows.Shapes;
using System.Windows.Threading;

namespace Pacman
{
  public partial class MainWindow : Window
  {
    public Game game;
    private DispatcherTimer dispatcherTimer;

    public MainWindow()
    {
      InitializeComponent();
      game = new Game();

      dispatcherTimer = new System.Windows.Threading.DispatcherTimer();
      dispatcherTimer.Tick += new EventHandler(dispatcherTimer_Tick);
      dispatcherTimer.Interval = new TimeSpan(0, 0, 0, 0, 500);
      dispatcherTimer.Start();

      this.KeyDown += new KeyEventHandler(MainWindow_KeyDown);
    }

    void MainWindow_KeyDown(object sender, KeyEventArgs e)
    {
      game.KeyPressed(e);
    }

    private void dispatcherTimer_Tick(object sender, EventArgs e)
```

```
  {
    game.PlayRound();
    if (!game.gameActive)
      dispatcherTimer.Stop();

    Paint();
    CommandManager.InvalidateRequerySuggested();
  }

...

  }
}
```

Listing 9-11: MainWindow.cs

In the MainWindow constructor, we create a new Game object as well as a DispatcherTimer object. We also add method MainWindow_KeyDown as a handler for the KeyDown event. This method updates the PacMan moving direction according to the key pressed by the user.

The dispatcher timer will tick every 500 milliseconds and will call method dispatcherTimer_Tick. This method plays one round of the game and then repaints the game maze on the canvas to reflect the new game state (by calling Paint()).

Here is the code for the Paint() method:

```
public void Paint()
{
  canvas.Children.Clear();

  var map = game.map;
  int BLOCK_WIDTH = 15;

  Rectangle background = new Rectangle();
  SolidColorBrush mySolidColorBrush1
    = new SolidColorBrush();
  mySolidColorBrush1.Color = Color.FromRgb(0, 0, 0);
  background.Fill = mySolidColorBrush1;
  background.StrokeThickness = 2;
  background.Stroke = Brushes.Black;
  background.Width = BLOCK_WIDTH * 28;
  background.Height = BLOCK_WIDTH * 32;
  Canvas.SetLeft(background, 0);
  Canvas.SetTop(background, 0);
  canvas.Children.Add(background);

  for (int i = 0; i < 32; i++)
    for (int j = 0; j < 28; j++)
    {
      if (map[i, j].entity != null)
      {
        if (map[i, j].entity?.GetType()
          .ToString().IndexOf("PacMan") >= 0)
```

```
{
  Rectangle r = new System.Windows.Shapes.Rectangle();
  SolidColorBrush mySolidColorBrush
    = new SolidColorBrush();
  mySolidColorBrush.Color
    = Color.FromRgb(255, 255, 0);
  r.Fill = mySolidColorBrush;
  r.StrokeThickness = 1;
  r.Stroke = Brushes.Black;
  r.Width = BLOCK_WIDTH;
  r.Height = BLOCK_WIDTH;
  Canvas.SetLeft(r, j * BLOCK_WIDTH);
  Canvas.SetTop(r, i * BLOCK_WIDTH);
  canvas.Children.Add(r);
}
else
{
  Rectangle r = new Rectangle();
  SolidColorBrush mySolidColorBrush
    = new SolidColorBrush();
  mySolidColorBrush.Color
    = Color.FromRgb(204, 0, 204);
  r.Fill = mySolidColorBrush;
  r.StrokeThickness = 1;
  r.Stroke = Brushes.Black;
  r.Width = BLOCK_WIDTH;
  r.Height = BLOCK_WIDTH;
  Canvas.SetLeft(r, j * BLOCK_WIDTH);
  Canvas.SetTop(r, i * BLOCK_WIDTH);
  canvas.Children.Add(r);
}
}
else
{
  if (map[i, j].type == BlockType.Wall)
  {
    Rectangle r = new Rectangle();
    SolidColorBrush mySolidColorBrush
      = new SolidColorBrush();
    mySolidColorBrush.Color
      = Color.FromRgb(255, 255, 255);
    r.Fill = mySolidColorBrush;
    r.StrokeThickness = 1;
    r.Stroke = Brushes.Black;
    r.Width = BLOCK_WIDTH;
    r.Height = BLOCK_WIDTH;
    Canvas.SetLeft(r, j * BLOCK_WIDTH);
    Canvas.SetTop(r, i * BLOCK_WIDTH);
    canvas.Children.Add(r);
  }
  else if (map[i, j].type == BlockType.Point)
  {
    Rectangle r = new Rectangle();
    SolidColorBrush mySolidColorBrush
```

```
            = new SolidColorBrush();
        mySolidColorBrush.Color
            = Color.FromRgb(255, 0, 0);
        r.Fill = mySolidColorBrush;
        r.StrokeThickness = 1;
        r.Stroke = Brushes.Black;
        r.Width = BLOCK_WIDTH;
        r.Height = BLOCK_WIDTH;
        Canvas.SetLeft(r, j * BLOCK_WIDTH);
        Canvas.SetTop(r, i * BLOCK_WIDTH);
        canvas.Children.Add(r);
    }
    else if (map[i, j].type == BlockType.Empty)
    {
        Rectangle r = new Rectangle();
        SolidColorBrush mySolidColorBrush
            = new SolidColorBrush();
        mySolidColorBrush.Color
            = Color.FromRgb(0, 255, 0);
        r.Fill = mySolidColorBrush;
        r.StrokeThickness = 1;
        r.Stroke = Brushes.Black;
        r.Width = BLOCK_WIDTH;
        r.Height = BLOCK_WIDTH;
        Canvas.SetLeft(r, j * BLOCK_WIDTH);
        Canvas.SetTop(r, i * BLOCK_WIDTH);
        canvas.Children.Add(r);
    }
  }
}

if (!game.gameActive)
{
  TextBlock textBlock = new TextBlock();
  textBlock.Text = "GAME OVER";
  textBlock.FontSize= 24;
  Color color = Color.FromRgb(255, 0, 0);
  textBlock.Foreground = new SolidColorBrush(color);
  Canvas.SetLeft(textBlock, 150);
  Canvas.SetTop(textBlock, 500);
  canvas.Children.Add(textBlock);
}
}
```
Listing 9-12: MainWindow.cs

Over a black background, we use white to paint the walls, red to paint the corridor blocks that contain points and green for the empty corridor blocks. We also use yellow for PacMan and magenta for the ghosts.

Now, let's see the PacMan class definition:

```
using System.Collections.Generic;

namespace Pacman
```

```
{
  public class PacMan : Entity
  {
    public PacMan(Game map, int x, int y)
    {
      this.game = map;
      this.type = EntityType.Pacman;
      this.x = x;
      this.y = y;
    }

    public override void Play()
    {
      var candidateBlocks = new List<Pair>();
      for (int i = x - 1; i <= x + 1; i++)
        for (int j = y - 1; j <= y + 1; j++)
        {
          if (i >= 0 && i < game.sizeX
              && j >= 0 && j < game.sizeY
              && !(i == x && j == y)
              && game.map[i, j].type != BlockType.Wall)
          {
            candidateBlocks.Add(new Pair(i, j));
          }
        }

      if (direction == Direction.Up
          && (candidateBlocks
          .Find(p => (p.x == x - 1 && p.y == y))) != null)
      {
        if (game.map[x-1, y].entity != null)
          game.gameActive = false;
        Move(x - 1, y);
      }
      else if (direction == Direction.Right
          && (candidateBlocks
          .Find(p => (p.x == x && p.y == y + 1))) != null)
      {
        if (game.map[x, y+1].entity != null)
          game.gameActive = false;
        Move(x, y + 1);
      }
      else if (direction == Direction.Down
          && (candidateBlocks
          .Find(p => (p.x == x + 1 && p.y == y))) != null)
      {
        if (game.map[x + 1, y].entity != null)
          game.gameActive = false;
        Move(x + 1, y);
      }
      else if (direction == Direction.Left
          && (candidateBlocks
          .Find(p => (p.x == x && p.y == y - 1))) != null)
      {
```

```
        if (game.map[x, y-1].entity != null)
          game.gameActive = false;
        Move(x, y - 1);
      }

      game.pacmanLocation.x = x;
      game.pacmanLocation.y = y;

      if (game.map[x, y].type == BlockType.Point)
      {
        game.map[x, y].type = BlockType.Empty;
        game.pointsLeft--;
        if (game.pointsLeft == 0)
          game.gameActive = false;
      }
    }
  }
}
```

Listing 9-13: PacMan.cs

The important stuff lies in the implementation of the `Play()` method. First of all, we find all neighbouring blocks that `PacMan` can move (that are not a wall actually) and we put them in a list of candidate blocks.

Next, depending on the `direction` currently selected by the user (using the arrow buttons) we move PacMan into the respective block, if available. Moving PacMan into a block means also updating the map with the position of PacMan, as well the elimination of the point (if any) in this block. The latter is performed by changing the type of the block to `Empty` and by reducing by one the remaining points in the game. If the points become zero then the game comes to an end.

The `Play()` method is an example of polymorphism at work. In `Game.cs`, on every loop we call the `Play()` method of each entity. The correct method is called depending on the type of the entity object (`PacMan` or `Ghost`).

Now let's move to the `Ghost` definition:

```
using System;
using System.Collections.Generic;
using System.Linq;

namespace Pacman
{
  public class Ghost : Entity
  {
    public Ghost(Game map, int x, int y)
    {
      this.game = map;
      this.type = EntityType.Ghost;
      this.x = x;
      this.y = y;
```

```
        }

        public override void Play()
        {
            var candidateBlocks = new List<Pair>();
            var distanceToPacman = new List<double>();

            for (int i = x - 1; i <= x + 1; i++)
                for (int j = y - 1; j <= y + 1; j++)
                {
                    if (i >= 0 && i < game.sizeX
                        && j >= 0 && j < game.sizeY
                        && !(i == x && j == y)
                        && game.map[i, j].type != BlockType.Wall)
                    {
                        candidateBlocks.Add(new Pair(i, j));
                        distanceToPacman
                            .Add(Math.Sqrt(Math.Pow(i - game.pacmanLocation.x, 2)
                                    + Math.Pow(j - game.pacmanLocation.y, 2)));
                    }
                }

            int minDistIn = distanceToPacman.IndexOf(distanceToPacman.Min());

            if (game.map[candidateBlocks.ElementAt(minDistIn).x,
                candidateBlocks.ElementAt(minDistIn).y]
                    .entity != null)
            {
                //move only if pacman is there
                if (game.map[candidateBlocks.ElementAt(minDistIn).x,
                    candidateBlocks.ElementAt(minDistIn).y]
                        .entity.type == EntityType.Pacman)
                {
                    //eat pacman
                    game.map[candidateBlocks.ElementAt(minDistIn).x,
                        candidateBlocks.ElementAt(minDistIn).y]
                            .entity = null;
                    game.gameActive = false;
                    Move(candidateBlocks.ElementAt(minDistIn).x,
                        candidateBlocks.ElementAt(minDistIn).y);
                }
            }
            else
            {
                Move(candidateBlocks.ElementAt(minDistIn).x,
                    candidateBlocks.ElementAt(minDistIn).y);
            }
        }
    }
}
```

Listing 9-14: Ghost.cs

In the `Play()` method, we again find the candidate neighbouring blocks for a move. Moreover, we calculate an array of the straight line distances of each candidate position to the PacMan entity.

After we have calculated the block with the smaller distance, the Ghost will move to this block, in an effort to get closer to PacMan. A Ghost may not move in a block where there is another Ghost, but it can step into the block where PacMan is located. In this case, PacMan is eaten by the Ghost and the game comes to an end.

This game has definitively lots more to be done. For instance, we have to implement the mode change where PacMan swallows the big pill and starts chasing the Ghost for a short period of time. Such functionality is left to reader as an exercise.

You can find this project in GitHub:

https://github.com/htset/csharp_oop_exercises/tree/master/Pacman

www.ingramcontent.com/pod-product-compliance
Lightning Source LLC
LaVergne TN
LVHW081759050326
832903LV00027B/2029